13

Things

Mentally

Strong

People

Don't Do

13 Things Mentally Strong People Don't Do

Take back your power, embrace change, face your fears & train your brain for happiness & success

The online phenomenon taking the world by storm

Amy Morin

Thorsons

HarperThorsons
An imprint of HarperCollins*Publishers*
1 London Bridge Street
London SE1 9GF

www.harpercollins.co.uk

First published in US by William Morrow, an imprint of
HarperCollins*Publishers* 2015
This UK edition published by HarperThorsons 2015

1 3 5 7 9 10 8 6 4 2

Designed by Jamie Lynn Kerner

A catalogue record of this book is
available from the British Library

ISBN 978-0-00-810593-8

Printed and bound in Great Britain by
Clays Ltd, St Ives plc

This book contains advice and information relating to health care. It is not intended
to replace medical advice and should be used to supplement rather than replace regular
care by your doctor. It is recommended that you seek your doctor's advice before
embarking on any medical program or treatment. All efforts have been made to assure
the accuracy of the information contained in this book as of the date of publication.
The publisher and the author disclaim liability for any medical outcomes that may
occur as a result of applying the methods suggested in this book.

The names and identifying details of many of the individuals discussed herein have
been changed to protect their privacy.

MIX
Paper from
responsible sources
FSC™ C007454

FSC is a non-profit international organisation established to promote
the responsible management of the world's forests. Products carrying
the FSC label are independently certified to assure consumers that they
come from forests that are managed to meet the social, economic
and ecological needs of present and future generations.

Find out more about HarperCollins and the environment at
www.harpercollins.co.uk/green

To all who strive to become better today than they were yesterday

CONTENTS

13

Things
Mentally
Strong
People
<u>Don't</u> Do

INTRODUCTION

When I was twenty-three, my mother died suddenly from a brain aneurysm. She'd always been a healthy, hardworking, vibrant woman who had loved life right up until her last minute on earth. In fact, I saw her the night before she died. We met at an auditorium to watch a high school basketball tournament. She was laughing, talking, and enjoying life like she always did. But just twenty-four hours later she was gone. The loss of my mother affected me deeply. I couldn't imagine going through the rest of my life without her advice, laughter, or love.

At the time, I was working as a therapist at a community mental health center, and I took a few weeks off to privately deal with my grief. I knew I couldn't be effective at helping other people unless I was able to productively deal with my own feelings. Becoming used to a life that no longer included my mother was a process. It wasn't easy, but I worked hard to get myself back on my feet. From my training as a therapist, I knew that time doesn't heal anything; it's how we deal with that time that determines the speed at which we heal. I understood that grief was the necessary process that would eventually alleviate my pain, so I allowed myself to feel sad, to get angry, and to fully accept what I'd truly lost when my mother passed away. It wasn't just that I missed her—it was also the painful realization that she would never be there again during the important events in my life and that she would never experience the things she'd looked forward to—like retire from her job and become a grandmother. With supportive friends and family, and my faith in God, I found a sense of peace; and as life went on, I was able to remember my mother with a smile, rather than with pangs of sadness.

A few years later, as we approached the third anniversary of my mother's death, my husband, Lincoln, and I discussed how to best honor her memory that weekend. Friends had invited us to watch a basketball game on Saturday evening. Coincidentally, the game was being played in the same auditorium where we'd last seen my mother. Lincoln and I talked about what it would be like to go back to the place where we'd seen her, just three years ago, on the night before she passed away.

We decided it could be a wonderful way to celebrate her life. After all, my memories of her that night were very good. We'd laughed, had a chance to talk about all kinds of things, and had an all-around great evening. My mother had even predicted my sister would get married to her boyfriend at the time—and a few years later that prediction came true.

So Lincoln and I returned to the auditorium and we enjoyed spending time with our friends. We knew it was what my mother would have wanted. It felt nice to go back and feel okay about being there. But just as I took a sigh of relief about my progress in dealing with my mother's death, my entire life was once again turned upside down.

After returning home from the basketball game, Lincoln complained of back pain. He'd broken several vertebrae in a car accident a few years prior, so back pain wasn't unusual for him. But just a few minutes later, he collapsed. I called for paramedics and they arrived within minutes and transported him to the hospital. I called his mother, and his family met me in the emergency room. I had no idea what could possibly be wrong with him.

After a few minutes in the emergency room waiting area, we

were called into a private room. Before the doctor even said a word, I knew what he was going to say. Lincoln had passed away. He'd had a heart attack.

On the same weekend that we honored the three-year anniversary of my mother's death, I now found myself a widow. It just didn't make any sense. Lincoln was only twenty-six and he didn't have any history of heart problems. How could he be here one minute and gone the next? I was still adjusting to life without my mother, and now I'd have to learn how to deal with life without Lincoln. I couldn't imagine how I would get through this.

Dealing with the death of a spouse is such a surreal experience. There were so many choices to be made at a time when I really wasn't in any shape to decide anything. Within a matter of hours, I had to start making decisions about everything from the funeral arrangements to the wording of the obituary. There wasn't any time to let the reality of the situation really sink in; it was completely overwhelming.

I was fortunate to have many people in my life who supported me. A journey through grief is an individual process, but loving friends and family certainly helped. There were times when it seemed to get a little easier and times when it would get worse. Just when I'd think I was getting better, I'd turn another corner to find overwhelming sadness waiting for me. Grief is an emotionally, mentally, and physically exhausting process.

There were so many things to feel sad about too. I felt sad for my husband's family, knowing how much they'd loved Lincoln. I felt sad about all the things Lincoln would never experience. And I was sad about all the things we'd never get to do together, not to mention, how much I missed him.

I took as much time off from work as I could. Those months are mostly a blur as I was focused on just putting one foot in front of the other every day. But I couldn't stay out of work forever. I was down to just one income and had to get back into the office.

After a couple of months, my supervisor called and asked about my plans to return to work. My clients had been told I would be out of the office indefinitely while I dealt with a family emergency. They weren't given any type of time frame about how long I'd be out, since we weren't really sure what was going to happen. But now, they needed an answer. I certainly wasn't done grieving, and I definitely wasn't "better," but I needed to go back to work.

Just like when I'd lost my mother, I had to allow myself time to experience the sorrow head-on. There was no ignoring it or pushing it away. I had to experience the pain while also proactively helping myself heal. I couldn't allow myself to stay stuck in my negative emotions. Although it would have been easy to pity myself or dwell on my past memories, I knew it wouldn't be healthy. I had to make a conscious choice to start down a long road to building a new life for myself.

I had to decide whether some of the goals Lincoln and I shared together were still going to be my goals. We'd been foster parents for a few years and had planned to eventually adopt a child. But did I still want to adopt a child as a single woman? I continued my work as a foster parent, providing mostly emergency and respite placements, for the next few years, but I wasn't sure I still wanted to adopt a child without Lincoln.

I also had to create new goals for myself now that I was alone. I decided to venture out and try new things. I got my motorcycle license and bought a motorcycle. I also began writing. At first it was mostly a hobby, but eventually it turned into a part-time job. I had to renegotiate new relationships with people as well by figuring out which of Lincoln's friends would remain my friends and what my relationship with his family would be like without him. Fortunately for me, many of his closest friends maintained friendships with me. And his family continued to treat me like part of their family.

About four years later, I was fortunate enough to find love

again. Or maybe I should say love found me. I was sort of getting used to life as a single person. But that all changed when I began dating Steve. We'd known each other for years and slowly our friendship turned into a relationship. Eventually, we started talking about a future together. Although I had never thought I'd get married again, with Steve it just seemed right.

I didn't want a formal wedding or a reception that parodied the ceremony I'd had with Lincoln. Although I knew my guests would be thrilled to see me marry again, I also knew it would conjure up pangs of sadness for people as they remembered Lincoln. I didn't want my wedding day to be a somber occasion, so Steve and I decided to have a nontraditional wedding. We eloped to Las Vegas and it was a completely joyous occasion that centered around our love and happiness.

About a year after we married, we decided to sell the house that Lincoln and I had lived in, and we moved a few hours away. We'd be closer to my sister and my nieces and it gave us an opportunity to have a fresh start. I got a job at a busy medical practice and we were looking forward to enjoying our future together. Just as life seemed to be going great, our road to happiness took another strange twist when Steve's father was diagnosed with cancer.

Initially, doctors predicted that his treatment could help keep the cancer at bay for several years. But after a few months, it was clear that he wasn't likely to survive one year, let alone several. He'd tried a few different options but nothing really worked. As time went on the doctors grew more perplexed by his lack of response to treatment. After about seven months, he'd run out of treatment options.

The news hit me like a ton of bricks. Rob was so full of life. He was the kind of guy who could always pull a quarter from behind a kid's ear and he told some of the funniest stories I have ever heard. Although he lived in Minnesota and we lived in Maine, we saw him often. Since he was retired, he had the availability to visit with us for weeks at a time and I'd always joked with him that he was my favorite houseguest—because he was basically our only houseguest.

He was also one of my biggest fans when it came to my writing. He read whatever I wrote, whether it was an article about parenting or a piece on psychology. Quite often, he'd call me with story ideas and suggestions.

Even though Rob was seventy-two, it felt like he was too young to be so sick. Right up until the previous summer he was motorcycling across the country, sailing around Lake Superior, and cruising the countryside with the top down in his convertible. But now he was too sick, and the doctors were clear—he was only going to get worse.

This time I had a different experience dealing with death. My mother's and Lincoln's deaths were completely unexpected and sudden. But this time, I had warning. I knew what was coming, and it filled me with a sense of dread.

I found myself thinking, *Here we go again*. I didn't want to go through such a staggering loss all over again. It just didn't seem right. I know plenty of people my age who haven't lost anyone, so why did I have to lose so many of my loved ones? I sat at the table thinking about how unfair it was, how hard it was going to be, and how much I wanted things to be different.

I also knew I couldn't let myself go down that road. After all, I'd been through this before and I'd be okay again. If I let myself fall into the trap of thinking my situation was worse than anyone else's, or if I convinced myself that I couldn't handle one more loss, it wasn't going to help. Instead, it would only hold me back from dealing with the reality of my situation.

It was at that moment that I sat down and wrote my list "13 Things Mentally Strong People Don't Do." They were the habits I'd fought so hard against to come out on the other side of my grief. They were the things that could hold me back from getting better, if I allowed them to take hold of me.

Not surprisingly, they were the same skills I was giving to the clients who entered my therapy office. But writing them down was something I needed to do to help me stay on track. It was a reminder that I could choose to be mentally strong. And I needed to be strong, because a few weeks after writing down that list, Rob passed away.

Psychotherapists are known for helping others build on their strengths, doling out tips on how they should act and what they can do to improve themselves. But when I created my list on mental strength, I decided to stray for a moment from what has become second nature to me. And focusing on what *not* to do has made all the difference. Good habits are important, but it's often our bad habits that prevent us from reaching our full potential. You can have all the good habits in the world, but if you keep doing the bad habits alongside the good ones, you'll struggle to reach your goals. Think of it this way: you're only as good as your worst habits.

Bad habits are like heavy weights that you drag around as you go about your day. They'll slow you down, tire you out, and frustrate you. Despite your hard work and talent, you'll struggle to reach your full potential when you've got certain thoughts, behaviors, and feelings holding you back.

Picture a man who chooses to go to the gym every day. He works out for almost two hours. He keeps a careful record of the exercises he performs so he can track his progress. Over the course of six months, he isn't noticing much of a change. He feels frustrated that he's not losing weight and gaining muscle. He tells his friends and family that it just doesn't make sense why he's not looking and feeling better. After all, he rarely ever misses a workout. What he leaves out of the equation is the fact that he enjoys a treat on his drive home from the gym every day. After all that exercise, he feels hungry and tells himself, "I've worked hard. I deserve a treat!" So each day, he eats one dozen donuts on his drive home.

Seems ridiculous, right? But we all are guilty of this kind of behavior. We work hard to do the things that we think will make us better, but we forget to focus on the things that might be sabotaging our efforts.

Avoiding these thirteen habits isn't just what will help you through grief. Getting rid of them will help you develop mental strength, which is essential to dealing with all life's problems—big or small. No matter what your goals are, you'll be better equipped to reach your full potential when you're feeling mentally strong.

WHAT IS MENTAL STRENGTH?

It's not that people are either mentally strong or mentally weak. We all possess some degree of mental strength, but there's always room for improvement. Developing mental strength is about improving your ability to regulate your emotions, manage your thoughts, and behave in a positive manner, despite your circumstances.

Just as there are those among us who are predisposed to develop physical strength more easily than others, mental strength seems to come more naturally to some people. There are several factors at play to determine the ease at which you develop mental strength:

- **Genetics**—Genes play a role in whether or not you may be more prone to mental health issues, such as mood disorders.

- **Personality**—Some people have personality traits that help them think more realistically and behave more positively by nature.

- **Experiences**—Your life experiences influence how you think about yourself, other people, and the world in general.

Obviously, you can't change some of these factors. You can't erase a bad childhood. You can't help it if you are genetically predisposed to ADHD. But that doesn't mean you can't increase your mental strength. Anyone has the power to increase mental strength by devoting time and energy on the self-improvement exercises throughout this book.

THE BASIS OF MENTAL STRENGTH

Imagine a man who feels nervous about social situations. To minimize his anxiety, he avoids starting conversations with his coworkers. The less he speaks with his coworkers, the less they initiate conversation with him. When he enters the break room and passes people in the hallway without anyone speaking to him, he thinks, *I must be socially awkward.* The more he thinks about how awkward he is, the more nervous he feels about starting conversations. As his anxiety increases, his desire to avoid his coworkers also increases. This results in a self-perpetuating cycle.

To understand mental strength, you have to learn how your thoughts, behaviors, and feelings are all intertwined, often working together to create a dangerous downward spiral as in the preceding example. This is why developing mental strength requires a three-pronged approach:

1. **Thoughts**—Identifying irrational thoughts and replacing them with more realistic thoughts.

2. **Behaviors**—Behaving in a positive manner despite the circumstances.

3. **Emotions**—Controlling your emotions so your emotions don't control you.

We hear it all the time: "Think positive." But optimism alone isn't enough to help you reach your full potential.

CHOOSE BEHAVIOR BASED ON BALANCED EMOTIONS AND RATIONAL THINKING

I'm terrified of snakes. Yet my fear is completely irrational. I live in Maine. We don't have a single poisonous snake in the wild. I don't see snakes very often, but when I do, my heart leaps into my throat and I'm tempted to run as fast as I can in the other direction. Usually, before I run away, I'm able to balance my sheer panic with rational thoughts that remind me that there's no logical reason to feel afraid. Once my rational thinking kicks in, I can walk by the snake—as long as he's a safe distance away. I still don't want to pick him up or pet him, but I can continue past him without letting my irrational fear interfere with my day.

We make our best decisions in life when we balance our emotions with rational thinking. Stop and think for a minute about how you behave when you're really angry. It's likely that you've said and done some things that you regretted later, because you were basing your actions on your emotions, not logic. But making choices based on rational thinking alone also doesn't make for good decisions. We are human beings, not robots. Our hearts and our heads need to work together to control our bodies.

Many of my clients question their ability to control their thoughts, emotions, and behavior. "I can't help the way I feel," they say. Or "I can't get rid of the negative thoughts that run through my head," and "I just can't get motivated to do what I want to accomplish." But with increased mental strength, it's possible.

THE TRUTH ABOUT MENTAL STRENGTH

There's a lot of misinformation and misconception about what it means to be mentally strong. Here are some of the truths about mental strength:

- *Being mentally strong isn't about acting tough.* You don't have to become a robot or appear to have a tough exterior when you're mentally strong. Instead, it's about acting according to your values.

- *Mental strength doesn't require you to ignore your emotions.* Increasing your mental strength isn't about suppressing your emotions; instead it's about developing a keen awareness of them. It's about interpreting and understanding how your emotions influence your thoughts and behavior.

- *You don't have to treat your body like a machine to be mentally strong.* Mental strength isn't about pushing your body to its physical limits just to prove you can ignore pain. It's about understanding your thoughts and feelings well enough that you can determine when to behave contrary to them, and when to listen to them.

- *Being mentally strong doesn't mean you have to be completely self-reliant.* Mental strength isn't about proclaiming that you don't ever need help from anyone or any type of higher power. Admitting you don't have all the answers, asking for help when you need it, and acknowledging that you can gain strength from a higher power is a sign of a desire to grow stronger.

- *Being mentally strong is not about positive thinking.* Thinking overly positive thoughts can be just as detrimental as thinking overly negative thoughts. Mental strength is about thinking realistically and rationally.

- *Developing mental strength isn't about chasing happiness.* Being mentally strong will help you to be more content in life, but it isn't about waking up every day and trying to force yourself to feel happy. Instead, it's about making the decisions that will help you reach your full potential.

- *Mental strength isn't just the latest pop psychology trend.* Just like the physical fitness world is filled with fad diets and fitness trends, the world of psychology is often filled with fleeting ideas about how to become your best self. Mental strength isn't a trend. The psychology field has been helping people learn how to change their thoughts, feelings, and behavior since the 1960s.

- *Mental strength isn't synonymous with mental health.* While the healthcare industry often talks in terms of mental health versus mental illness, mental strength is different. Just like people can still be physically strong even if they have a physical health ailment like diabetes, you can still be mentally strong even if you have depression, anxiety, or other mental health problems. Having a mental illness doesn't mean you're destined to have bad habits. Instead, you can still choose to develop healthy habits. It may require more work, more focus, and more effort, but it's very possible.

THE BENEFITS OF MENTAL STRENGTH

It's often easy to feel mentally strong when life is going well, but at times problems arise. A job loss, a natural disaster, an illness in the family, or a death of a loved one is sometimes inevitable. When you're mentally strong, you'll be more prepared to deal with life's challenges. Benefits of increasing your mental strength include:

- **Increased resilience to stress**—Mental strength is helpful in everyday life, not just in the midst of a crisis. You'll become better equipped to handle problems more efficiently and effectively, and it can reduce your overall stress level.

- **Improved life satisfaction**—As your mental strength increases, your confidence will also increase. You'll behave according to your values, which will give you peace of mind, and you'll recognize what's really important in your life.

- **Enhanced performance**—Whether your goal is to be a better parent, to increase your productivity at the office, or to perform better on the athletic field, increasing your mental strength will help you reach your full potential.

HOW TO DEVELOP MENTAL STRENGTH

You'll never become an expert at anything by simply reading a book. Athletes don't become elite competitors after reading about their sport nor do top musicians increase their musical abilities by simply watching other performers play. They also have to practice.

The following thirteen chapters aren't meant to be a checklist that you either do or don't do. They are a description of habits that everyone falls prey to sometimes. It's meant to help you find better ways to cope with life's challenges so you can avoid these pitfalls. It's about growing, improving, and striving to become a little better than you were yesterday.

CHAPTER 1

THEY DON'T WASTE TIME FEELING SORRY FOR THEMSELVES

Self-pity is easily the most destructive of the non-pharmaceutical narcotics; it is addictive, gives momentary pleasure and separates the victim from reality.
—JOHN GARDNER

During the weeks that followed Jack's accident, his mother couldn't stop talking about the "horrible incident." Every day she recounted the story about how both of Jack's legs were broken when he was hit by a school bus. She felt guilty that she wasn't there to protect him, and seeing him in a wheelchair for several weeks was almost more than she could bear.

Although doctors had predicted a complete recovery, she repeatedly warned Jack that his legs may never fully heal. She wanted him to be aware that he may not be able to play soccer or run around like the other kids ever again, just in case there was a problem.

Although his doctors had medically cleared him to return to school, his parents decided that Jack's mother would quit her job and homeschool him for the remainder of the year. They felt that seeing and hearing school buses each day might trigger too many bad memories. They also wanted to spare him from having to watch idly from his wheelchair as his friends played at recess. They hoped that staying home would help Jack heal faster, both emotionally and physically.

Jack usually completed his homeschool work in the mornings and he spent his afternoons and evenings watching TV and playing video games. Within a few weeks, his parents noticed that his mood seemed to change. A normally upbeat and happy child, Jack became irritable and sad. His parents grew concerned that the accident may have traumatized him even more than they'd imagined. They pursued therapy in hopes it could help Jack deal with his emotional scars.

Jack's parents took him to a well-known therapist with expertise in childhood trauma. The therapist had received the referral from Jack's pediatrician, so she knew a little bit about Jack's experience prior to meeting him.

When Jack's mother wheeled him into the therapist's office, Jack stared silently at the floor. His mother began by saying, "We're having such a hard time since this terrible accident. It's really ruined our lives and caused a lot of emotional problems for Jack. He's just not the same little boy."

To his mother's surprise, the therapist didn't respond with sympathy. Instead she enthusiastically said, "Boy, have I been looking forward to meeting you, Jack! I've never met a kid who could beat a school bus! You have to tell me, how did you manage to get into a fight with a school bus and win?" For the first time since the accident Jack smiled.

Over the next few weeks, Jack worked with his therapist on making his own book. He appropriately named it, How to Beat a School Bus. *He created a wonderful story about how he managed to fight a school bus and escape with only a few broken bones.*

He embellished on the story by describing how he grabbed hold of the muffler, swung himself around, and protected the majority of his body from getting hit by the bus. Despite the exaggerated details, the main part of the story remained the same—he survived because he's a tough kid. Jack concluded his book with a self-portrait. He drew himself sitting in a wheelchair wearing a superhero cape.

The therapist included Jack's parents in the treatment. She helped them see how fortunate they were that Jack survived with only a few broken bones. She encouraged his parents to stop feeling sorry for Jack. She recommended they treat him like a mentally and physically tough kid who was capable of overcoming great adversity. Even if his legs didn't heal properly, she wanted them to focus on what Jack could still accomplish in life, not what the accident would prevent him from being able to do.

The therapist and Jack's parents worked with the school faculty and staff to prepare for Jack's return to school. In addition to the special accommodations he'd need because he was still in a wheelchair, they wanted to ensure that the other students and teachers didn't pity Jack. They arranged for Jack to share his book with his classmates so that he could tell them how he beat the school bus and show them that there was no reason to feel sorry for him.

SELF-PITY PARTY

We all experience pain and sorrow in life. And although sadness is a normal, healthy emotion, dwelling on your sorrow and misfortune is self-destructive. Do you respond positively to any of the points below?

❐   You tend to think your problems are worse than anyone else's.

❐   If it weren't for bad luck, you're pretty sure you'd have none at all.

❐   Problems seem to add up for you at a much faster rate than anyone else.

❐   You're fairly certain that no one else truly understands how hard your life really is.

❑   You sometimes choose to withdraw from leisure activ-
     ities and social engagements so you can stay home and
     think about your problems.

❑   You're more likely to tell people what went wrong
     during your day rather than what went well.

❑   You often complain about things not being fair.

❑   You struggle to find anything to be grateful for sometimes.

❑   You think that other people are blessed with easier lives.

❑   You sometimes wonder if the world is out to get you.

Can you see yourself in some of the examples above? Self-pity
can consume you until it eventually changes your thoughts and
behaviors. But you can choose to take control. Even when you
can't alter your circumstances, you can alter your attitude.

WHY WE FEEL SORRY FOR OURSELVES

If self-pity is so destructive, why do we do it in the first place?
And why is it sometimes so easy and even comforting to indulge
in a pity party? Pity was Jack's parents' defense mechanism to protect their son and themselves from future dangers. They chose
to remain focused on what he couldn't do as a way to shield him
from having to face any more potential problems.

Understandably, they worried about his safety more than ever.
They didn't want him to be out of their sight. And they were
concerned about the emotional reaction he might have to seeing
a school bus again. It was only a matter of time before the pity
poured on Jack turned into his own self-pity.

It's so easy to fall into the self-pity trap. As long as you feel sorry for yourself, you can delay any circumstances that will bring you face-to-face with your real fears, and you can avoid taking any responsibility for your actions. Feeling sorry for yourself can buy time. Instead of taking action or moving forward, exaggerating how bad your situation is justifies why you shouldn't do anything to improve it.

People often use self-pity as a way to gain attention. Playing the "poor me" card may result in some kind and gentle words from others—at least initially. For people who fear rejection, self-pity can be an indirect way of gaining help by sharing a woe-is-me tale in hopes it will attract some assistance.

Unfortunately, misery loves company, and sometimes self-pity becomes a bragging right. A conversation can turn into a contest, with the person who has experienced the most trauma earning the badge of victory. Self-pity can also provide a reason to avoid responsibility. Telling your boss how bad your life is may stem from hopes that less will be expected from you.

Sometimes self-pity becomes an act of defiance. It's almost as if we assume that something will change if we dig in our heels and remind the universe that we deserve better. But that's not how the world works. There isn't a higher being—or a human being for that matter—who will swoop in and make sure we're all dealt a fair hand in life.

THE PROBLEM WITH FEELING SORRY FOR YOURSELF

Feeling sorry for yourself is self-destructive. It leads to new problems and can have serious consequences. Instead of feeling grateful that Jack survived the accident, his parents worried about what the accident took away from them. As a result, they allowed the accident to take away even more.

That's not to say they weren't loving parents. Their behavior stemmed from a desire to keep their son safe. However, the more they pitied Jack, the more negatively it affected his mood.

Indulging in self-pity hinders living a full life in the following ways:

- *It's a waste of time.* Feeling sorry for yourself requires a lot of mental energy and does nothing to change the situation. Even when you can't fix the problem, you can make choices to cope with life's obstacles in a positive way. Feeling sorry for yourself won't move you any closer to a solution.

- *It leads to more negative emotions.* Once you allow it to take hold, self-pity will ignite a flurry of other negative emotions. It can lead to anger, resentment, loneliness, and other feelings that fuel more negative thoughts.

- *It can become a self-fulfilling prophecy.* Feelings of self-pity can lead to living a pitiful life. When you feel sorry for yourself, it's unlikely you'll perform at your best. As a result, you may experience more problems and increased failures, which will breed more feelings of self-pity.

- *It prevents you from dealing with other emotions.* Self-pity gets in the way of dealing with grief, sadness, anger, and other emotions. It can stall your progress from healing and moving forward because self-pity keeps the focus on why things should be different rather than accepting the situation for what it is.

- *It causes you to overlook the good in your life.* If five good things and one bad thing happen in a day, self-pity will cause you to focus only on the negative. When you feel sorry for yourself, you'll miss out on the positive aspects of life.

- *It interferes with relationships.* A victim mentality is not an attractive characteristic. Complaining about how bad your life is will likely wear on people rather quickly. No one ever says, "What I really like about her is the fact that she always feels sorry for herself."

STOP FEELING SORRY FOR YOURSELF

Remember the three-pronged approach to achieving mental strength? To alleviate feelings of self-pity, you need to change your pitiful behavior and forbid yourself from indulging in pitiful thoughts. For Jack, this meant that he couldn't spend all his time at home playing video games and watching TV. He needed to be around other kids his age and return to some of his previous activities that he was still able to do, like go to school. His parents also changed their thinking and began to view Jack as a survivor rather than a victim. Once they changed their thoughts about their son and the accident, they were able to exchange self-pity with gratitude.

BEHAVE IN A MANNER THAT MAKES IT HARD TO FEEL SORRY FOR YOURSELF

Four months after Lincoln died, his family and I were facing what should have been his twenty-seventh birthday. I had been dreading that day for weeks because I had no idea how we'd pass the time. My cartoon bubble pictured us sitting around in a circle sharing a box of Kleenex and talking about how unfair it was that he never reached his twenty-seventh birthday.

When I finally worked up the courage to ask my mother-in-law how she planned to spend the day, without missing a beat she said, "What do you think about skydiving?" The best part was, she was serious. And, I had to admit, jumping out of a perfectly good airplane did seem like a much better idea than the pity party I'd imagined. It felt like the perfect way to honor Lincoln's adventurous spirit. He'd always enjoyed meeting new people, going new places, and experiencing new things. It wasn't unusual for him to head off on a spontaneous weekend trip, even if it meant he'd be flying the red-eye home and would have to go to work as soon as he stepped off the overnight flight. He'd say that one day of feeling tired at work was well worth the memories we'd created. Skydiving was something Lincoln would have loved to do so it seemed like an appropriate way to celebrate his life.

It's impossible to feel sorry for yourself when you're jumping out of an airplane—unless of course, you don't have a parachute. Not only did we have a great time, but our skydiving experience led to an annual tradition. Every year on Lincoln's birthday, we choose to celebrate his love of life and adventure. It's led to some interesting experiences—from swimming with sharks to riding mules into the Grand Canyon. We've even taken flying trapeze lessons.

Each year, the whole family becomes involved in Lincoln's birthday adventure. Some years, Lincoln's grandmother watches from the sidelines with her camera, but two years ago, at the age of eighty-eight, she was first in line to go ziplining high above the trees. Even though I'm remarried, it's a tradition we've continued, and my husband, Steve, even participates with us. It's become a day we actually look forward to each year.

Our choice to spend the day doing something enjoyable isn't about ignoring our grief or masking our sadness. It's about making a conscious choice to celebrate life's gifts and refusing to behave in a pitiful manner. Instead of pitying ourselves for what we lost, we choose to feel grateful for what we had.

When you notice self-pity creeping into your life, make a conscious effort to do something contrary to how you feel. You don't have to jump out of a plane to ward off feelings of self-pity. Sometimes, small behavioral changes can make a big difference. Here are some examples:

- *Volunteer to help a worthy cause.* It will take your mind off your problems and you can feel good that you've helped support someone else. It's hard to feel sorry for yourself when you're serving hungry people in a soup kitchen or spending time with elderly residents in a nursing home.

- *Perform a random act of kindness.* Whether you mow the neighbor's lawn or donate pet food to a local animal shelter, doing a good deed can help bring more meaning to your day.

- *Do something active.* Physical or mental activity will help you focus on something other than your misfortune. Exercise, sign up for a class, read a book, or learn a new hobby, and your behavior change can help shift your attitude.

The key to changing your feelings is finding which behaviors will extinguish your feelings of self-pity. Sometimes it's a process of trial and error because the same behavioral change won't work for everyone. If what you're doing now isn't working, try something new. If you never take a step in the right direction, you'll stay right where you are.

REPLACE THOUGHTS THAT ENCOURAGE SELF-PITY

I once witnessed a fender bender in a grocery store parking lot. Two cars were backing up at the same time and their rear bumpers collided. The collision appeared to cause only minor damage to each vehicle.

I watched as one driver jumped out of his vehicle and said, "Just what I needed. Why do these things always happen to me? As if I didn't already have enough to deal with today!"

Meanwhile, the other driver stepped out of his vehicle shaking his head. In a very calm voice he said, "Wow, we're so lucky that no one got hurt. What a great day it is when you can get into an accident and walk away from it without a single injury."

Both men experienced the exact same event. However, their perception of the event was completely different. One man viewed himself as a victim of horrible circumstance while the other man viewed the event as good fortune. Their reaction was all about their differences in perception.

You can view the events that happen in your life in many different ways. If you choose to view circumstances in a way that says, "I deserve better," you'll feel self-pity often. If you choose to look for the silver lining, even in a bad situation, you'll experience joy and happiness much more often.

Almost every situation has a silver lining. Ask any kid what the best part about having divorced parents is and most of them will say, "I get more presents at Christmas!" Obviously, there isn't much good that arises from divorce, but getting twice as many presents is one small aspect of divorce that some kids rather enjoy.

Reframing the way you look at a situation isn't always easy, especially when you're feeling like the host of your own pity party. Asking yourself the following questions can help change your negative thoughts into more realistic thoughts:

- *What's another way I could view my situation?* This is where the "glass half empty or glass half full" thinking comes in. If you're looking at it from the glass-half-empty angle, take a moment to think about how someone looking from a glass-half-full perspective might view the same situation.

- *What advice would I give to a loved one who had this problem?* Often, we're better at handing out words of encouragement to other people rather than to ourselves. It's unlikely you'd say to someone else, "You've got the worst life ever. Nothing ever goes right." Instead, you'd hopefully offer some kind words of assistance such as, "You'll figure out what to do, and you'll make it through this. I know you will." Take your own words of wisdom and apply them to your situation.

- *What evidence do I have that I can get through this?* Feeling sorry for ourselves often stems from a lack of confidence in our ability to handle problems. We tend to think that we'll never get through something. Remind yourself of times when you've solved problems and coped with tragedy in the past. Reviewing your skills, support systems, and past experiences can give you an extra boost of confidence that will help you stop feeling sorry for yourself.

The more you indulge in thoughts that willfully delude yourself about your situation, the worse you'll feel.

Common thoughts that lead to feelings of self-pity include things such as:

- *I can't handle one more problem.*

- *Good things always happen to everyone else.*

- *Bad things always happen to me.*

- *My life just gets worse all the time.*

- *No one else has to deal with this stuff.*

- *I just can't catch a break.*

You can choose to catch your negative thoughts before they spiral out of control. Though replacing overly negative thoughts with more realistic ones takes practice and hard work, it's very effective in decreasing feelings of self-pity.

If you think, *Bad things* always *happen to me,* create a list of good things that have happened to you as well. Then, replace your original thought with something more realistic like, *Some bad things happen to me, but plenty of good things happen to me as well.* This doesn't mean you should turn something negative into an unrealistically positive affirmation. Instead, strive to find a realistic way to look at your situation.

EXCHANGE SELF-PITY FOR GRATITUDE

Marla Runyan is a very accomplished woman. She has a master's degree, she's written a book, and she's competed in the Olympics. She even became the first American woman to finish the 2002 New York Marathon with an astounding time of 2 hours, 27 minutes. What makes Marla particularly extraordinary is that she's accomplished all these feats despite the fact that she's legally blind.

At age nine, Marla was diagnosed with Stargardt's disease, a form of macular degeneration that affects children. As her vision deteriorated, Marla discovered her love for running. Over the years, Marla has proved herself to be one of the fastest runners in the world, even though she's never actually been able to see the finish line.

Initially, Marla became an accomplished athlete in the Paralympics. She competed in 1992 and then again in 1996. Not only did she earn a total of five gold medals and one silver medal, she also set several world records. But Marla didn't stop there.

In 1999, she entered the Pan American Games and she won the 1,500-meter race. In 2000, she became the first legally blind athlete to ever compete in the Olympics. She was the first American to cross the finish line in the 1,500-meter race and she placed eighth overall.

Marla doesn't see her blindness as a disability. In fact, she chooses to view it as a gift that allows her to become successful in both long- and short-distance races. In discussing her blindness in her book, *No Finish Line: My Life as I See It,* Marla writes, "It not only has forced me to prove my competence but also pushed me to achieve. It has given me gifts, such as will and commitment that I use every day." Marla doesn't focus on what her vision loss took from her. Instead, she chooses to feel grateful for what her vision impairment actually gave her.

While feeling sorry for yourself is about thinking *I deserve better,* gratitude is about thinking *I have more than I deserve.* Experiencing gratitude requires some extra effort, but it isn't hard. Anyone can learn to become more grateful by developing new habits.

Start to acknowledge other people's kindness and generosity. Affirm the good in the world and you will begin to appreciate what you have.

You don't have to be rich, wildly successful, or have the perfect life to feel grateful. A person who earns $34,000 a year may think he doesn't have much money but he is actually among the richest 1 percent of people in the world. If you're reading this book, it means you're more fortunate than the nearly one billion people in the world who can't read, many of whom will be stuck in a life of poverty.

Look for those little things in life that you can so easily take for granted and work toward increasing your feelings of gratitude. Here are a few simple habits that can help you focus on what you have to be grateful for:

- *Keep a gratitude journal.* Each day write down at least one thing you're grateful for. It could include being grateful for simple pleasures, like having clean air to breathe or seeing the sun shine, or major blessings like your job or family.

- *Say what you're grateful for.* If you aren't likely to keep up with writing in a journal, make it a habit to say what you're grateful for. Find one of life's gifts to be grateful for each morning when you wake up and each night before you go to sleep. Say the words out loud, even if it's just to yourself, because hearing the words of gratitude will increase your feelings of gratitude.

- *Change the channel when you're experiencing self-pity.* When you notice that you're starting to feel sorry for yourself, shift your focus. Don't allow yourself to continue thinking that life isn't fair or that life should be different. Instead, sit down and list the people, circumstances, and experiences in life that you can be thankful for. If you keep a journal, refer to it and read it whenever self-pity begins to set in.

- *Ask others what they're grateful for.* Strike up conversations about gratitude to help you discover what other people feel thankful for. Hearing what others feel grateful for can remind you of more areas of your life that deserve gratitude.

- *Teach kids to be grateful.* If you're a parent, teaching your children to be grateful for what they have is one of the best ways to keep your own attitude in check. Make it a habit each day to ask your children what they're grateful for. Have everyone in the family write down what they're feeling grateful for and place it in a gratitude jar or hang it on a bulletin board. This will give your family a fun reminder to incorporate gratitude into your daily lives.

GIVING UP SELF-PITY WILL MAKE YOU STRONGER

Jeremiah Denton served as a U.S. naval aviator during the Vietnam War. In 1965, his plane was shot down and he was forced to eject from his aircraft. He was captured by the North Vietnamese and was taken as a prisoner of war.

Commander Denton and the other officers maintained command over their fellow prisoners even as they were beaten, starved, and tortured on a daily basis. Commander Denton was often placed in solitary confinement for urging other prisoners to resist the North Vietnamese attempts to gain information from them. But that didn't stop Commander Denton. He devised strategies to communicate with the other prisoners by using signs, tapping on walls, and coughing in sequence.

Ten months after his capture, he was chosen to participate in a televised interview that was used as propaganda. While answering questions, he pretended as though the bright lights from the cameras were bothering his eyes as he began blinking T-O-R-T-U-R-E in Morse code to secretly send the message that he and his fellow prisoners were being mistreated by their captors. Throughout the interview, he continued to express his support for the U.S. government.

He was released in 1973 after seven years in captivity. When he stepped off the plane as a free man, he said, "We are honored to have had the opportunity to serve our country under difficult circumstances. We are profoundly grateful to our commander in chief and to our nation for this day. God bless America." After retiring from the military in 1977, he was elected to serve as senator for Alabama.

Despite being placed in the worst circumstances imaginable, Jeremiah Denton didn't waste time feeling sorry for himself. Instead, he maintained his composure and focused on doing whatever he could to manage the situation. Even when he was released, he chose to feel grateful that he was able to serve his country, rather than pity himself for the time he'd lost.

Researchers studied the differences that occur when people focus on their burdens versus focusing on what they're grateful for. Simply acknowledging a few things you feel grateful for each day is a powerful way to create change. In fact, gratitude not only impacts your psychological health, it can also affect your physical health. A 2003 study published in the *Journal of Personality and Social Psychology* found:

- *People who feel gratitude don't get sick as often as others.* They have better immune systems and report fewer aches and pains. They have lower blood pressure and they exercise more often than the general population. They take better care of their health, sleep longer, and even report feeling more refreshed upon waking.

- *Gratitude leads to more positive emotions.* People who feel grateful experience more happiness, joy, and pleasure on a daily basis. They even feel more awake and energetic.

- *Gratitude improves social lives.* Grateful people are more willing to forgive others. They behave in a more outgoing fashion and feel less lonely and isolated. They are also more likely to help other people and to behave in a generous and compassionate manner.

TROUBLESHOOTING AND COMMON TRAPS

If you allow self-pity to take hold when you're dealing with stress, you'll put off working on a solution. Watch out for red flags that you're allowing yourself to feel self-pity and take a proactive approach to change your attitude at the first sign of feeling sorry for yourself.

WHAT'S HELPFUL

Giving yourself a reality check so you don't exaggerate how bad the situation really is

Replacing overly negative thoughts about your situation with more realistic thoughts

Choosing to actively problem-solve and work on improving your situation

Getting active and behaving in a way that makes you less likely to feel sorry for yourself, even when you don't feel like it

Practicing gratitude every day

WHAT'S NOT HELPFUL

Allowing yourself to believe that your life is worse than most other people's lives

Indulging in exaggeratedly negative thoughts about how difficult your life is

Remaining passive about the situation and focusing only on how you feel, rather than what you can do

Declining to participate in experiences and activities that could help you feel better

Staying focused on what you don't have rather than what you do have

CHAPTER 2

THEY DON'T GIVE
AWAY THEIR POWER

When we hate our enemies, we are giving them power over us: power over our sleep, our appetites, our blood pressure, our health, and our happiness.
—DALE CARNEGIE

Lauren was convinced her overbearing, meddling mother-in-law was going to ruin her marriage, if not her entire life. Although she had thought her mother-in-law, Jackie, was annoying in the past, it wasn't until she and her husband had two children together that she found her to be unbearable.

Jackie usually made several unannounced visits each week, and she often stayed for several hours at a time. Lauren found those visits to be intrusive on their family time because she only had so much time with her girls between the time she came home from work and the time they went to bed.

But what really bothered Lauren was the way Jackie always tried to undermine her authority with the girls. Jackie would often say things to the children like "You know, a little TV won't hurt you. I don't know why your mother always says you can't watch it" or "I'd let you have dessert but your mother's convinced sugar is bad for your health." She sometimes lectured Lauren about her "new age parenting" and reminded her that she allowed her children to watch TV and eat sweets and they seemed to turn out just fine.

Lauren always responded to Jackie's comments with a polite nod and a smile, but on the inside, she was seething. She grew resentful toward Jackie and she often took it out on her husband. But whenever Lauren complained to her husband about his mother, he'd say something like "Well, you know how she is," or "Just ignore her comments. She means well." Lauren found comfort in complaining to her girlfriends who had affectionately named Jackie the "monster-in-law."

But one week, everything seemed to come to a head when Jackie suggested Lauren should start exercising more because she looked like she had gained a little weight. That comment pushed Lauren over the edge. She stormed out of the house and spent the night at her sister's. The next day, she still didn't feel ready to go home. She was afraid she'd have to hear a lecture from Jackie about how she shouldn't have left. It was at that point Lauren knew she had to get help or her marriage might be in jeopardy.

Lauren initially sought counseling to learn anger management skills to help her respond less angrily to her mother-in-law's comments. However, after a few therapy sessions, she was able to see that she needed to work on being more proactive in preventing problems, not just less reactive toward Jackie's comments.

I asked Lauren to complete a pie chart that showed how much time and energy she focused on various areas of her life, such as work, sleep, leisure, family, and time with her mother-in-law. I then asked her to complete a second pie chart that showed how many hours she physically spent doing each activity. When she was done with the second pie chart, she was surprised to see how much her time and energy were out of proportion. Although she only physically spent about five hours a week with her mother-in-law, she was devoting at least an additional five hours thinking and talking about her disdain for her. This exercise helped her see how she was giving her mother-in-law power over many areas of her life. When *she could have devoted her energy to nurturing her relationship with her husband or caring for her children, she was often thinking about how much she disliked Jackie.*

Once Lauren recognized how much power she was giving Jackie, she chose to start making some changes. She worked with her husband on setting healthy boundaries for their family. Together, they established rules that would help them limit the influence Jackie had on their family. They told Jackie that she could no longer make unannounced visits several times per week. Instead, they would invite her over for dinner when they wanted to visit with her. They also informed her that she could no longer undermine Lauren's authority as a mother, and if she did, she'd be asked to leave. Lauren also chose to stop complaining about Jackie. She recognized that venting to her friends and her husband only fueled her frustration and wasted her time and energy.

Slowly, but surely, Lauren began to feel like she was getting her life and her house back. She no longer dreaded Jackie's visits once she recognized she didn't have to tolerate rude or disrespectful behavior in her home. Instead, she could control what went on under her own roof.

EMPOWERING OTHER PEOPLE TO HAVE POWER OVER YOU

Giving other people the power to control how you think, feel, and behave makes it impossible to be mentally strong. Do any of the points below sound familiar?

- ❐ You feel deeply offended by any criticism or negative feedback you receive, regardless of the source.

- ❐ Other people have the ability to make you feel so angry that you say and do things you later regret.

- ❐ You've changed your goals based on what other people have told you that you should be doing with your life.

❏ The type of day you're going to have depends on how other people behave.

❏ When other people try to guilt you into doing something, you reluctantly do it, even if you don't want to.

❏ You work hard to ensure other people see you in a positive light because much of your self-worth depends on how others perceive you.

❏ You spend a lot of time complaining about people and circumstances that you don't like.

❏ You often complain about all the things you "have to" do in life.

❏ You go to great lengths to avoid uncomfortable emotions, like embarrassment or sadness.

❏ You have difficulty setting boundaries, but then feel resentful toward people who take up your time and energy.

❏ You hold a grudge when someone offends you or hurts you.

Can you see yourself in any of the above examples? Retaining your power is about being confident in who you are and the choices you make, despite the people around you and the circumstances you're in.

WHY WE GIVE AWAY OUR POWER

Lauren was clear that she really wanted to be a nice person, and she thought that being a good wife meant tolerating her mother-in-law at all costs. She felt it would be disrespectful to ask her mother-in-law not to come over and she was hesitant to speak up when her feelings were hurt. She'd been raised to "turn the other cheek" when someone treated her poorly. But with help, she was able to see that setting healthy boundaries wasn't being mean or disrespectful. Instead, setting limits on what was allowed in her own home was healthy for her family and less taxing on her mental strength.

Anytime you don't set healthy emotional and physical boundaries for yourself, you risk giving away your power to other people. Perhaps you don't dare say no when your neighbor asks for a favor. Or maybe you dread receiving a phone call from a friend who constantly complains, but you continue to pick up on the first ring. Each time you avoid saying no to something you really don't want, you give away your power. If you don't make any attempt to get your needs met, you'll give people permission to take things away from you.

A lack of emotional boundaries can be equally problematic. If you don't like the way someone treats you, yet you don't stand up for yourself, you give that person power over your life.

THE PROBLEM WITH GIVING AWAY YOUR POWER

Lauren allowed her mother-in-law to control what sort of an evening she was going to have. If Jackie showed up, Lauren felt angry and bitter about the fact that she wasn't getting to spend quality time with her children. On the days Jackie didn't come to her home, Lauren felt much more relaxed. She allowed Jackie's behavior to interfere with her relationship with her children, as well as her marriage.

Instead of spending her spare time talking to her husband and her friends about enjoyable subjects, she wasted her energy complaining about Jackie. She even found herself sometimes volunteering to work late because she wasn't excited about going home when she knew Jackie was going to be there. The longer she gave her power to Jackie, the more helpless she became about fixing it.

There are many problems with giving away your power:

- *You depend on others to regulate your feelings.* When you give away your power, you become completely dependent upon other people and external circumstances to regulate your emotions. Life often becomes like a roller coaster—when things are going well, you'll feel good; but when your circumstances change, your thoughts, feelings, and behavior will shift.

- *You let other people define your self-worth.* If you give others the power to determine your self-worth, you'll never feel worthy enough. You'll only be as good as someone else's opinion of you and you will never be able to receive enough praise or positive feedback to meet your needs if you depend on others to feel good about yourself.

- *You avoid addressing the real problem.* Giving away your power lends itself to helplessness. Rather than focus on what you can do to improve the situation, you'll find an excuse to justify your problems.

- *You become a victim of your circumstances.* You'll become a passenger in your own life rather than a driver. You'll say other people make you feel bad or force you to behave in a manner you don't like. You'll blame others instead of accepting responsibility for your choices.

- *You become highly sensitive to criticism.* You'll lack the ability to evaluate criticism. Instead, you'll take anything anyone says to heart. You'll give much more power to other people's words than those words deserve.

- *You lose sight of your goals.* You won't be able to build the kind of life you want when you allow other people to be in control of your goals. You can't work toward your goals successfully when you give other people the power to get in your way and interfere with your progress.

- *You ruin relationships.* If you don't speak up when people hurt your feelings or you allow them to infringe on your life in an unwelcomed manner, you'll likely grow resentful toward them.

RECLAIM YOUR POWER

Without confidence in who you are, your entire self-worth may depend on how others feel about you. What if you offend people? What if they don't like you anymore? If you choose to put up healthy boundaries, you may receive some backlash. But if you have a strong enough sense of self-worth, you'll learn that you can tolerate the repercussions.

Lauren learned that she could be firm with her mother-in-law, while still behaving respectfully. Although she was terrified of confrontation, Lauren and her husband explained their concerns to Jackie together. Initially, Jackie was offended when they told her she could not come over every night. And Jackie tried to argue when they explained that she would not be allowed to make rude comments about Lauren's rules for the children. But, over time, Jackie accepted that she had to follow these rules if she wanted to come into their home.

IDENTIFY PEOPLE WHO HAVE TAKEN YOUR POWER

Steven McDonald is an incredible example of someone who chose not to give away his power. While working as a New York City police officer in 1986, Officer McDonald stopped to question some teenagers about some recent bicycle thefts. One of the fifteen-year-olds in question took out a gun and shot Officer McDonald in the head and neck. The shots paralyzed him from the neck down.

Miraculously, Officer McDonald survived. He spent eighteen months in the hospital recuperating and learning how to live as a quadriplegic. At the time of the accident, he'd only been married eight months, and his wife was six months pregnant.

Remarkably, Officer McDonald and his wife chose not to focus on all that had been taken away from them by this teenage boy. Instead, they made a conscious choice to forgive him. In fact, a few years after his injury, the officer's assailant called him from jail to apologize. Officer McDonald not only accepted his apology, but he also told him that he hoped someday they could travel the country together sharing their story with the hope they could prevent other acts of violence. Officer McDonald never got the chance to do that, however, because three days after his assailant was released from prison, the young man was killed in a motorcycle accident.

So Officer McDonald set out on his mission to spread his message about peace and forgiveness on his own. "The only thing worse than a bullet in my spine would have been to nurture revenge in my heart," he says in the book *Why Forgive?* He may have lost his physical mobility in that attack, but he didn't give that violent incident or his assailant the power to ruin his life. He's now a highly sought after speaker who teaches love, respect, and forgiveness. Officer McDonald is an inspirational example of someone who, despite being the victim of a senseless act of violence, chose not to waste time giving his assailant more power.

Choosing to forgive someone who has hurt you, either emotionally or physically, doesn't mean you have to excuse the other person's behavior, but letting go of your anger frees you to focus your energy on a more worthwhile cause.

If you've spent most of your life feeling like a victim of your circumstances, it takes hard work to recognize that you have the power to choose your own path in life. The first step is to develop self-awareness by identifying when you blame external circumstances and other people for how you think, feel, and behave. Take a close look at the people you are devoting your time and energy toward. Are they the people you want to receive it? If not, you may be giving them more power than you think they deserve.

Each second you spend commiserating with coworkers about how unfair your boss is, you are giving your boss more power. Every time you tell your friends how controlling your mother-in-law is, you give her a little more power over you. Resolve to stop giving people your time and energy if you don't want them to play a big role in your life.

REFRAME YOUR LANGUAGE

Sometimes retaining your power means changing the way you look at the situation. Examples of language that indicates you're giving away your power include:

- "My boss *makes* me so mad." You may not like your boss's behavior, but does he really *make* you feel angry? Perhaps your boss behaves in a manner that you don't like and it may influence how you feel, but he's not forcing you to feel anything.

- "My boyfriend left me because I'm *not good enough*." Are

you really not good enough or is that just one person's opinion? If you took a poll of a hundred people, it's not likely that they'd all come to that same consensus. Just because one person thinks something, it doesn't make it true. Don't give one person's opinion of you the power to determine who you are.

- "My mom *makes* me feel really bad about myself because she's always so critical of me." As an adult, are you obligated to listen to your mother make critical statements about you over and over? Just because she makes comments you don't like, does it really have to lower your self-esteem?

- "I *have* to invite my in-laws over for dinner every Sunday night." Do your in-laws really force you to do that or is that a choice you make because it's important to your family?

THINK BEFORE YOU REACT

Rachel brought her sixteen-year-old daughter to me for therapy because her daughter refused to listen to her. No matter what she told her daughter to do, she just wouldn't do it. I asked Rachel how she reacted when her daughter refused to follow her directions. Out of exasperation, she told me, she yelled and argued with her. Each time her daughter said, "No!," Rachel yelled, "Do it!"

Rachel didn't realize it, but she was giving her daughter a lot of power. Every minute that she argued with her daughter was one more minute her daughter could put off cleaning her room. Each time she lost her temper, Rachel gave away some of her power. Instead of controlling her daughter's behavior, Rachel was giving her daughter power to control her.

If someone says something you don't like, and you yell or begin to argue, you give those words you don't like even more power. Make a conscious choice to think about how you want to behave before you react to other people. Every time you lose your cool, you give that other person your power. Here are some strategies to help you stay calm when you're tempted to react negatively:

- *Take deep breaths.* Frustration and anger cause physical reactions within the body—an increased rate of breathing, an elevated heart rate, and sweating to name a few. Taking slow, deep breaths can relax your muscles and decrease the physiological response, which in turn can decrease your emotional reactivity.

- *Excuse yourself from the situation.* The more emotional you feel, the less rational you'll think. Learn to recognize your personal warning signs of anger—such as shaking or feeling flushed—and remove yourself from the situation before you lose your cool. This may mean saying, "I am not willing to talk about that right now," or it may mean walking away.

- *Distract yourself.* Don't try solving a problem or addressing an issue with someone when you're feeling overly emotional. Instead, distract yourself with an activity, like walking or reading, to help you calm down. Getting your mind off what's bothering you, even for a few minutes, can help you calm down so you can think more rationally.

EVALUATE FEEDBACK CRITICALLY

Not long before she released an album that sold over ten million copies, Madonna received a rejection letter from the president of

Millennium Records that said, "The only thing missing from this project is the material." Had Madonna allowed that letter to define her singing and songwriting abilities, she might have given up. But fortunately, she kept looking for opportunities in the music industry. Soon after that rejection letter, she landed a record deal that launched her career. Within a couple of decades, Madonna was recognized by the Guinness Book of World Records as the bestselling female recording artist of all time. She holds numerous other records, including the top-touring female artist of all time, and she's ranked second on the Billboard Hot 100 All-Time Top Artists—second only to the Beatles.

Almost every successful person likely has a similar story of rejection. In 1956, Andy Warhol tried to give one of his paintings to the Museum of Modern Art, but they declined to accept it even for free. Fast-forward to 1989, and his paintings had become so successful that he earned his own museum. The Andy Warhol Museum is the largest museum in the United States dedicated to a single artist. Clearly, everyone has an opinion, but successful people don't allow one person's opinion to define them.

Retaining your power is about evaluating feedback to determine if it has any validity. While criticism can sometimes open our eyes to how others perceive us so we can make positive change—a friend points out a bad habit, or a spouse helps you see your selfish behavior—at other times, criticism is a reflection of the critic. Angry people may choose to offer harsh criticism quite regularly just because it relieves their stress. Or individuals with low self-esteem may feel better about themselves only when they put other people down. So it's important to really consider the source before making any decisions about how you want to proceed.

When you receive criticism or feedback from others, wait a

beat before responding. If you're upset or emotionally reactive, take the time to calm down. Then ask yourself these questions:

- *What evidence is there that this is true?* For example, if your boss says you are lazy, look for evidence of times when you haven't worked very hard.

- *What evidence do I have this isn't true?* Look for times when you have put in a lot of effort and have been a hard worker.

- *Why might this person be giving me this feedback?* Take a step back and see if you can find out why this person may be giving you negative feedback. Is it based on the small sampling of your behavior that the person has witnessed? For example, if your boss only watched you work on a day where you were coming down with the flu, she may decide that you aren't very productive. Her conclusion may not be accurate.

- *Do I want to change any of my behavior?* There may be times where you choose to change your behavior because you agree with the other person's criticism. For example, if your boss says you're lazy, maybe you'll decide that you haven't been putting in as much effort at the office as you could. So you decide to start showing up early and staying late because it's important to you to be a good worker. Just remember, though, that your boss isn't forcing you to do anything different. You are choosing to create change because you want to, not because you have to.

Keep in mind that one person's opinion of you doesn't make it true. You can respectfully choose to disagree and move on without devoting time and energy into trying to change the other person's mind.

RECOGNIZE YOUR CHOICES

There are very few things in life you *have* to do, but often we convince ourselves we don't have a choice. Instead of saying, "I *have* to go to work tomorrow," remind yourself that it's a choice. If you choose not to go to work, there will be consequences. Perhaps you won't get paid. Or maybe you'll risk losing your job altogether. But it's a choice.

Simply reminding yourself that you have a choice in everything you do, think, and feel can be very freeing. If you've spent most of your life feeling like a victim of your circumstances, it takes hard work to recognize that you have the power to create the kind of life you want to live.

TAKING BACK YOUR POWER WILL MAKE YOU STRONGER

You don't get to be named one of the most powerful people in the world by giving away your power. Just ask Oprah Winfrey. She grew up in extreme poverty and was sexually abused by several people throughout her childhood. She bounced between living with her mother, father, and grandmother, and as a teenager, she frequently ran away from home. She became pregnant at age fourteen, but the infant died shortly after birth.

During her high school years, she began working at a local radio station. She worked her way through several media jobs, and eventually, she landed a job as a TV news anchor. But she was later fired from the position.

She didn't allow one person's opinion of her on-air suitability to stop her, however. She went on to create her own talk show and by the age of thirty-two, her show became a national hit. By the age of forty-one, she had a reported net worth of over $340 million. Oprah has started her own magazine, radio show, and TV network and has coauthored five books. She's even won an Academy Award. She's started a multitude of charities to help people in need, including a leadership academy for girls in South Africa.

Oprah didn't let her childhood or her former employer take away her power. A woman who was once teased because she was so poor she wore potato sacks as dresses was named one of the world's most powerful women by both CNN and *Time*. Statistically, her upbringing would have predicted a poor prognosis. But Oprah refused to be a statistic. She chose to define who she was going to be in life by not giving away her power.

When you decide that no one else has the power to control how you feel, you'll experience empowerment. Here are some other ways how retaining your power will help you become mentally strong:

- *You'll develop a better sense of who you are when you're able to make choices based on what's best for you instead of what will prevent the most repercussions.*

- *When you take responsibility for your own behavior, you'll become accountable for your progress toward your goals.*

- *You will never be pressured into doing something that you don't want to do based on guilt trips or what you think other people want you to do.*

- *You'll be able to devote your time and energy to things you choose.* You won't have to blame other people for wasting your time or ruining your day.

- *Retaining your personal power reduces your risk of depression, anxiety, and other mental health issues.* Many mental health problems are linked to a sense of hopelessness and helplessness. When you decide not to give other people and external circumstances the power to control how you feel and behave, you gain more power over your mental health.

When you hold a grudge, those feelings of anger and resentment do nothing to lessen the other person's life. Instead, harboring anger and resentment gives that person more power to interfere with your quality of life. Choosing to forgive allows you to take back your power, not just over your psychological health, but also over your physical health. Research shows some of the health benefits of forgiveness include the following:

- *Forgiveness reduces your stress.* Over the years, many studies have shown that holding a grudge keeps your body in a state of stress. When you practice forgiveness, your blood pressure and heart rate decrease.

- *Choosing to forgive increases your tolerance to pain.* In a 2005 study of patients with chronic low back pain, anger increased psychological distress and decreased a person's tolerance to pain. A willingness to forgive was associated with increased pain tolerance.

- *Unconditional forgiveness can help you to live longer.* A 2012 study published in the *Journal of Behavioral Medicine* discovered that when people were only willing to forgive others under certain conditions—like the other person apologized or promised to never repeat the same behavior—their risk of dying early actually increased.

You don't have any control over whether someone will apologize. Waiting to forgive people until they say they're sorry gives them control over not just your life, but perhaps even your death.

TROUBLESHOOTING AND COMMON TRAPS

Monitor your personal power and look for ways in which you are voluntarily giving it away. It takes hard work, but increasing your mental strength requires you to retain every ounce of personal power for yourself.

WHAT'S HELPFUL

Using language that acknowledges your choice such as, "I'm choosing to . . ."

Setting healthy emotional and physical boundaries with people

Behaving proactively by making conscious choices about how you'll respond to others

Taking full responsibility for how you choose to spend your time and energy

Choosing to forgive individuals regardless of whether they seek to make amends

Willingness to examine feedback and criticism without jumping to conclusions

WHAT'S NOT HELPFUL

Using language that implies you're a victim, such as "I *have* to do this," or "My boss *makes* me so mad"

Feeling anger and resentment toward people you allow to infringe on your rights

Reacting to others and then blaming them for the way you handled yourself

Doing things you don't want to do and then blaming others for "making" you do it

Choosing to hold a grudge and harbor anger and resentment

Allowing feedback and criticism to control how you feel about yourself

CHAPTER 3

THEY DON'T SHY AWAY FROM CHANGE

It's not that some people have willpower and some don't . . .
It's that some people are ready to change and others are not.
—JAMES GORDON

Richard entered my therapy office because he wasn't making much progress in managing his physical health. At the age of forty-four, he was seventy-five pounds overweight and had recently been diagnosed with diabetes.

Shortly after his diagnosis, he'd met with a nutritionist and learned about the diet changes he'd need to make to lose weight and manage his blood sugar. Initially, he tried eliminating all the junk food he had always eaten so regularly. He'd gone so far as to throw away all the ice cream, cookies, and sugary soft drinks he had in his home. But within two days, he found himself buying more sweets and resorting to his old habits.

He was also aware that he'd need to increase his activity level if he wanted to get healthier. After all, he was no stranger to exercise. Back in high school, he'd been a star athlete on the football field and the basketball court. But these days, he spent the majority of his time sitting behind a computer. He worked long hours and wasn't sure how he'd find the time to exercise. He'd purchased a gym membership, but he'd only gone to the gym twice. He usually came home from work exhausted, and he already felt like he wasn't spending enough time with his wife and children.

Richard told me that he really wanted to get healthier. But he felt frustrated. Despite understanding the risks of being overweight and the dangers of not managing his diabetes, he just couldn't motivate himself to change his unhealthy habits.

It was clear that he was trying to change too much too fast, which is a recipe for failure. I recommended he choose one thing to change at a time and for the first week, he said he'd give up the cookies he usually ate at his desk during the afternoon. It was important to find something to replace that habit with—and he decided he would try snacking on carrot sticks instead.

I also recommended he gain support to help him become healthier. He agreed to attend a diabetes support group. And over the next few weeks we discussed strategies to help get his family involved. His wife attended a few therapy sessions with him, and she began to understand steps she could take to help Richard improve his health. She agreed not to buy as much junk food when she went grocery shopping, and she began working with Richard on finding healthier recipes for their meals.

We also discussed a realistic exercise schedule. Richard said that almost every day he left the house planning to go to the gym after work, but he always talked himself out of it and went straight home. We decided he'd start by going to the gym three days a week and he scheduled those three days ahead of time. He also kept a list of all the reasons why going to the gym was a good idea in the car. On the days when he began thinking that he should just go home instead of going to the gym, he read over his list as a reminder about why going to the gym was the best choice, even if he didn't feel like it.

Over the next two months, Richard began losing weight. But his blood sugar was still fairly high. He admitted that he was still eating a lot of junk food in the evenings while he watched TV. I encouraged him to find ways to make it less convenient for him to reach for sugary snacks, so he decided that he'd keep the sweet treats downstairs in the basement. Then, when he wandered into the kitchen in the evenings, he'd be more likely to reach for a *healthy snack. If he still wanted cookies, he'd have to think about whether he wanted to go down to the basement to get them and most of the time, he found that he was more motivated to reach for a healthier snack. As soon as he started making progress, he found it easier to make more changes. Eventually, he was able to feel more inspired to lose weight and manage his blood sugar.*

TO CHANGE OR NOT TO CHANGE

Although it's often easy to say you want to change, successfully making a change is hard. Our thoughts and emotions often prevent us from creating behavioral change, even when it will improve our lives.

Many people shy away from making changes that can drastically improve their lives. See if any of the following apply to you:

❑   You tend to justify a bad habit by convincing yourself what you're doing isn't "that bad."

❑   You experience a lot of anxiety about changes to your routine.

❑   Even when you're in a bad situation, you worry that making a change might make things worse.

❑   Whenever you attempt to make a change, you struggle to stick with it.

❑   When your boss, family, or friends make changes that affect you, it's difficult for you to adapt.

❑   You think a lot about making changes but put off doing anything different until later.

❒ You worry that any changes you make aren't likely to last.

❒ The thought of stepping outside your comfort zone just seems too scary.

❒ You lack the motivation to create positive change because it's too hard.

❒ You make excuses for why you can't change, like "I'd like to exercise more, but my spouse doesn't want to go with me."

❒ You have difficulty recalling the last time you purposely tried to challenge yourself to become better.

❒ You hesitate to do anything new because it just seems like too big of a commitment.

Do any of the above examples sound familiar? Although circumstances can change quickly, humans often change at a much slower pace. Choosing to do something different requires you to adapt your thinking and your behavior, which will likely bring up some uncomfortable emotions. But that doesn't mean you should shy away from change.

WHY WE SHY AWAY FROM CHANGE

Initially, Richard tried to change too much too fast and he quickly became overwhelmed. Whenever he thought, *This is going to be too hard,* he allowed himself to give up. As soon as he began seeing some positive results, however, his thoughts became more positive and it was easier for him to stay motivated. Many people shy away from change because they think that doing something different is too risky or uncomfortable.

...e different types of change, some you might
...n others:

- ...**..or-nothing change**—Some changes are incremental while others are basically all or nothing. Deciding to have a child, for example, isn't something you can do in steps. Once you have that baby, your life has irrevocably changed.

- **Habit change**—You can choose to either get rid of bad habits, like sleeping too late, or you can choose to create good habits, like exercising five times a week. Most habit changes allow you to try something new for a little while, but you can always revert back to your old habits.

- **Trying-something-new change**—Change sometimes involves trying something new or mixing up your daily routine, like volunteering at a hospital or taking violin lessons.

- **Behavioral change**—Sometimes there are behavioral changes that don't necessarily constitute a habit. For example, maybe you want to commit to going to all of your child's sports games or maybe you want to behave friendlier.

- **Emotional change**—Not all change is tangible. Sometimes it's emotional. For example, if you want to feel less irritable all the time, you'll need to examine the thoughts and behaviors that contribute to your irritability.

- **Cognitive change**—There may be ways in which you want to change your thinking as well. Perhaps you want to think less about the past or maybe decrease worrisome thoughts.

READINESS FOR CHANGE

New Year's resolutions are commonly broken, because we try to make changes based on a date and not because we're really ready. And if you aren't ready to create change, you likely won't be successful at maintaining it. Even changing one small habit, like deciding you'll floss your teeth every day or giving up your bedtime snack, requires a certain level of commitment.

THE FIVE STAGES OF CHANGE

1. **Precontemplation**—When people are precontemplative, they don't yet identify any need to change. Richard was precontemplative about making any changes to his health for years. He avoided going to the doctor, he refused to step on a scale, and he dismissed any comments his wife made when she expressed concern about his health.

2. **Contemplation**—People who are actively contemplative are considering the pros and cons of making a change. When I first saw Richard, he was contemplative. He was aware that not changing his eating habits could have serious consequences, but he was also not yet certain how to go about creating change.

3. **Preparation**—This is the stage where people prepare to make a change. They establish a plan with concrete steps that identify what they are going to do differently. Once Richard moved into the preparation stage, he scheduled days to work out and chose one snack to swap for something healthier.

4. **Action**—This is where the concrete behavioral change takes place. Richard started going to the gym and swapped his afternoon cookies for carrots.

5. **Maintenance**—This often overlooked step is essential. Richard needed to plan ahead so he could maintain his lifestyle changes when he faced obstacles, like holidays or vacations.

FEAR

When I met Andrew, he was stuck in a low-paying job that didn't challenge him. He had a college degree—and the student loans to prove it—but he was working in a field that didn't use any of his skills. There was little opportunity for advancement.

A few months prior to our first session, he'd gotten into a car accident. Not only was his car totaled, but he'd racked up some hefty medical bills. He was underinsured in terms of both his health and his vehicle, and he was experiencing serious financial problems.

Despite feeling a lot of stress about his financial situation, Andrew was afraid to apply for new jobs. He worried that he might not like a different job, and he lacked confidence in his skills. He also dreaded the thought of getting used to a new office, a new boss, and different coworkers.

I helped Andrew examine the pros and cons of a job change. Once Andrew developed a budget, he was able to examine the facts of the situation. Staying at his current job would make it impossible to pay for his bills each month. Even without a single unexpected expense, he would be at least $200 shy of paying his bills. Facing this reality gave Andrew the motivation he needed to begin applying for new jobs. The fear of not being able to pay his bills had to outweigh the fear of getting a new job that paid better.

Just like Andrew, many people worry that doing something different may make things even worse. Maybe you don't like the house you're living in, but you worry that a new home could have even bigger problems. Or maybe you worry about ending a relationship because you are afraid you won't ever find anyone better. So you convince yourself to keep things the same, even if you're not happy.

AVOIDING DISCOMFORT

Many people associate change with discomfort. And often, they underestimate their ability to tolerate the discomfort that accompanies a behavioral change. Richard knew what changes he needed to make to improve his health, but he didn't want to give up foods he liked or feel the pain that accompanies a workout. And he worried that losing weight meant he'd have to be hungry. He dreaded all those realities, but he didn't realize that these slight discomforts were just that, and nothing worse. It wasn't until he began gaining confidence in his ability to tolerate discomfort that he truly felt like making further changes.

GRIEF

Tiffany came to therapy because she wanted to change her spending habits. Her shopping had become out of control, and she felt stressed because she was carrying around huge credit card balances. She didn't want to keep spending but at the same time, she didn't want to change. When we discussed some of her concerns about what would happen if she tried to stick to a budget, she discovered that she didn't want to give up time with her friends, because she and her girlfriends often spent Saturday afternoons shopping together. She thought the only way to curb her spending meant giving up time with her friends, which she feared would lead to loneliness.

Doing something different means giving something up. And there's often a grief associated with leaving something behind. To spare ourselves this grief, we can convince ourselves not to change. Tiffany would have rather held on to her girls' day at the mall than avoid financial ruin.

THE PROBLEM WITH SHYING AWAY FROM CHANGE

Shying away from change can have serious consequences. In Richard's case, continuing his current habits would likely take a serious toll on his health. The longer he delayed making change, the more irreversible damage he was likely to suffer.

But avoiding change doesn't always have just physical consequences. Remaining stagnant can also interfere with personal growth in other areas of your life.

- *Staying the same often equals getting stuck in a rut.* Life can get pretty boring if you don't do anything differently. A person who simply decides to keep things as mundane and low-key as possible isn't likely to experience a rich, full life and might become depressed.

- *You won't learn new things.* The world will change with or without you. Don't think that your choice not to change will prevent anyone else from embracing change. You'll risk being left in the dust if you choose to keep doing everything the same for the rest of your life.

- *Your life may not get better.* If you don't change, you can't make your life better. Many problems that are waiting to be solved require you to do something different. But if you aren't willing to try something new, those issues are likely to remain unresolved.

- *You won't challenge yourself to develop healthier habits.* It's easy to develop bad habits. Breaking bad habits requires a willingness to try something new.

- *Other people will outgrow you.* "My husband isn't the same man I married thirty years ago." I hear this all the time in my office, and my response is usually, "Let's hope not." I hope everyone grows and changes over the course of thirty years. If you are unwilling to challenge yourself and improve, others may grow bored with you.

- *The longer you wait the harder it gets.* Do you think it's easier to quit smoking after your first cigarette or after twenty years of smoking? The longer you keep the same habits, the harder they can be to break. Sometimes people put off change until the right time. They say things like "I'll look for a new job when things calm down" or "I'll worry about losing weight after the holidays." But, often, the perfect time to do something never arises. The longer change gets delayed, the harder it is to do.

ACCEPT CHANGE

I first learned of Mary Deming from one of her close friends who couldn't stop saying enough good things about her. And when I heard Mary's story, I began to understand why. But it wasn't until I spoke with her that it truly hit me.

When Mary was eighteen, her mother was diagnosed with breast cancer. Three short years later, her mother passed away. Following her mother's death, Mary admits she buried her head in the sand. She says she vacillated between feeling sorry for herself—her father had passed away when she was a teen so she felt it was unfair she was an "orphan" at 21—and busying herself with as much activity as possible so she didn't have to face the reality of her situation.

But in 2000, at the age of fifty—the same age her father had been when he passed away—Mary began thinking about her own mortality. That same year, as a high school teacher, Mary was asked to chaperone a school-sponsored fund-raiser for cancer research. Chaperoning that event provided Mary with an opportunity to meet with other people who had lost loved ones to cancer and the fund-raiser ignited her passion to make a difference. She began participating in fund-raising events for cancer research.

Initially, she joined the American Cancer Society's "Relay for Life" as her first fund-raiser walk. Then, in 2008, she joined the three-day sixty-mile walk sponsored by Susan G. Komen that was specifically aimed at raising money for breast cancer. Mary had always been a competitive person and when she saw how much money other people were able to raise, she kicked it into high gear and single-handedly raised $38,000, one thousand dollars for each year her mother had been gone.

But instead of patting herself on the back for a job well done, Mary credits the people in her small town with helping her raise the funds. And her fund-raising endeavors made her recognize that raising money for cancer research was near and dear to her neighbors' hearts. She began to do some research and she discovered that her home state of Connecticut had the second highest rate of breast cancer in the nation. And that sparked an idea.

Mary decided to start her own nonprofit agency to raise money, and she got the entire community involved. She named her organization Seymour Pink, after her town of Seymour, Connecticut. Each October—breast cancer awareness month—the town makes sure everyone has an opportunity to "see more pink." Businesses decorate with pink. Pink banners honoring survivors and memorializing loved ones who have lost their battle to breast cancer are hung on the light posts throughout the town. Homes are decorated with pink ribbons and balloons.

Over the years, Mary has raised almost a half million dollars for breast cancer–related causes. Her organization donates some money for cancer research and also provides direct financial support to families who are affected by cancer. Not only does Mary not take any of the credit—she only boasts about how wonderful her community members are who participate in her fund-raisers—but she also fails to mention her personal triumphs. I only learned about the obstacles she overcame because someone else told me.

Just three years into her fund-raising efforts, Mary was in a severe car accident. A traumatic brain injury left her with significant speech and cognitive issues. But even a serious car accident couldn't hold someone like Mary back. She went to speech therapy eight times a week and was determined to get back to raising money for breast cancer patients and research. At a time when most people would have retired, Mary said, "I'm not going out like that." She knew it would be a long road to recovery but she didn't believe in quitting. It took her five years, but by 2008, she returned to her job as a high school science teacher and resumed her fund-raising efforts.

Mary didn't set out to change the world. Instead, she focused on what she could do to make a difference. If you start by changing your life, you can begin to make a difference in the lives of other people. Mother Teresa said, "I alone cannot change the world, but I can cast a stone across the waters to create many ripples." Mary

Deming didn't set out to change the entire world either, but she sure has changed a lot of lives.

IDENTIFY THE PROS AND CONS OF CHANGING

Create a list of what is good about staying the same and what is bad about staying the same. Then, create a list about the potentially good and bad outcomes of making a change. Don't simply make your decision based on the sheer number of pros versus cons. Instead, examine the list. Read it over a few times and think about the potential consequences of changing versus staying the same. If you're still considering change, this exercise can help you move closer to making a decision.

There's no need to change for the sake of change. Moving to a new home, starting a new relationship, or switching jobs aren't inherently going to increase your mental strength. Instead, it's important to pay close attention to the reasons why you want to change so you can determine whether the decision is about doing what's ultimately best for you.

If you're still ambivalent, create a behavioral experiment. Unless you're dealing with an all-or-nothing change, try something new for one week. After you've done it for a week, evaluate your progress and motivation. Decide if you want to continue with the change or not.

DEVELOP AN AWARENESS OF YOUR EMOTIONS

Pay attention to the emotions that are influencing your decision as well. When you think about making a change, how do you feel? For example:

• Are you nervous that the change won't last?

- Do you feel exhausted at the sheer thought of doing something different?

- Are you worried about your ability to follow through with the change?

- Are you scared things may get worse?

- Are you sad that you'll have to give something up?

- Are you uncomfortable even admitting a problem exists?

Once you identify some of your emotions, you can decide whether it makes sense to act contrary to those emotions. Richard, for example, felt a variety of emotions. He was nervous about committing to something new. He was feeling guilty that he may need to give up time with his family to exercise and he was worried that he wouldn't be successful at managing his health. Despite all that, he was even more fearful about what would happen to him if he didn't make a change.

Don't allow your emotions to make the final decision. Sometimes you have to be willing to change, even when you don't "feel like it." Balance your emotions with rational thinking. If you're terrified of doing something new, and it really won't make a big difference in your life, you may decide it's not worth putting yourself through the stress of change. But, if you can rationally identify how change will be best for you in the long term, it may make sense to tolerate the discomfort.

MANAGE NEGATIVE THOUGHTS

Look for unrealistically negative thoughts that may be influencing you. Once you've started to make changes, the way you think about the process can also greatly affect how motivated you'll be to keep going. Be on the alert for these types of thoughts that will tempt you to shy away from change:

- *This will never work.*

- *I can't handle doing something different.*

- *It will be too hard.*

- *It'll be too stressful to give up the things I like.*

- *What I'm doing now isn't that bad.*

- *There's no sense in trying because I tried something like that before and it didn't help.*

- *I don't deal with change well.*

Just because you think it will be difficult doesn't mean you shouldn't do it. Often, some of the best things in life come from our ability to conquer a challenge through hard work.

CREATE A SUCCESSFUL PLAN FOR CHANGE

Preparing for the change can be the most important step. Create a plan for how you'll implement the change and how you'll stick to it. Once you have a plan in place, then you can implement the behavioral change one small step at a time.

Initially, Richard told himself he needed to lose seventy-five pounds. Thinking about that huge number however, overwhelmed him. He just didn't think it was possible. He started each day with the best of intentions, but by the evening, he slid back into his old habits. It wasn't until he began focusing on what he could do *today* that he was able to start making helpful behavioral changes. By establishing smaller goals, such as losing five pounds, he was able to create action steps that he could do each day. He kept a food journal, packed his lunch instead of dining out, and went for a short walk with his family on the days he didn't go to the gym.

Unless you're dealing with an all-or-nothing type of change, you can create change in incremental steps. Prepare for making the change with these steps:

- *Create a goal for what you would like to accomplish in the next thirty days.* Sometimes people try to change everything all at once. Identify one goal that you want to focus on first and establish a realistic expectation for what you'd like to see change in one month's time.

- *Establish concrete behavior changes you can make to reach that goal each day.* Identify at least one step you can take each day to move closer to your goal.

- *Anticipate obstacles along the way.* Make a plan for how you will respond to specific challenges that you're likely to encounter. Planning ahead can help you stay on track.

- *Establish accountability.* We do best when we establish some type of accountability for our progress. Enlist the help of friends and family who can provide support and check in with you about your progress. Be accountable to yourself by writing down your progress daily.

- *Monitor your progress.* Determine how you'll keep track of your progress. Keeping a record of your efforts and daily achievements can help you stay motivated to maintain changes.

BEHAVE LIKE THE PERSON YOU WANT TO BECOME

If your goal is to be more outgoing, behave in a friendly manner. If you want to be a successful salesperson, study how successful salespeople behave and then do what they do. You don't necessarily have to wait until you feel like it or until the right time comes; start changing your behavior now.

Richard wanted to be healthier, so he needed to behave like a healthy person. Eating a healthy diet and engaging in more physical activity were two things Richard could start doing to get closer to his goals.

Clearly identify the type of person you'd like to be. Then, be proactive about becoming that person. So often I hear, "I wish I could have more friends." Don't wait for friends to come to you; start acting like a friendly person now and you can develop new friendships.

EMBRACING CHANGE WILL MAKE YOU STRONGER

Judge Greg Mathis was raised in the projects of Detroit during the 1960s and 1970s. As a teenager, he was arrested many times, and he dropped out of school to join a gang. At the age of seventeen, while incarcerated at a juvenile detention center, his mother was diagnosed with colon cancer. Mathis was offered early probation as a result of her illness and promised his dying mother he'd turn his life around once and for all.

His probation terms required him to maintain a job, and he began working at McDonald's. He was accepted to Eastern Michigan University and went on to law school. Due to his criminal history, he wasn't able to get a job as a lawyer, but that didn't stop him from finding ways to help the city of Detroit. He became manager of the Detroit Neighborhood City Halls. Around the same time, he and his wife established Young Adults Asserting Themselves, a nonprofit agency that helped young people find employment. A few years later, Mathis decided to run for judge. Although his opponents reminded the community of his criminal background, the people of Detroit believed Mathis was a changed man. Mathis was elected the youngest judge in Michigan's history after beating out the twenty-year incumbent. Judge Mathis soon gained Hollywood attention and in 1999, he began a successful TV show where he settles small-claims disputes.

Once a criminal himself, Judge Mathis now donates much of his time and energy to helping young people make better decisions in their lives. He tours the country offering Youth and Education Expos that encourage young people to make the best choices they can for their future. He's received multiple awards and commendations for his ability to inspire young people to avoid making the same mistakes he made in his life.

Sometimes change results in a complete transformation that could alter the entire course of your life. So often, when people become committed to create change in one area of their lives, like pay off their debt, before they know it, they're also losing weight and their marriages improve. Positive change leads to increased motivation and increased motivation leads to more positive change. Embracing change is a two-way street.

TROUBLESHOOTING AND COMMON TRAPS

Unfortunately, your life will change whether you want it to or not. Change created by job loss, death of a loved one, a friend moving away, or kids moving out are all a part of life. When you practice adapting to the small changes, you'll be better prepared to deal with the large inevitable changes that come your way.

Pay attention to the way you handle change. Watch out for

warning signs that you may be avoiding important change that could ultimately improve your life. Although change can feel uncomfortable, you won't be able to increase your mental strength unless you're willing to grow and improve.

WHAT'S HELPFUL

Evaluating your readiness to change with an open mind

Setting a realistic time frame to establish and reach your goals

Balancing your emotions and rational thoughts to help you make a decision about whether to do something different

Willingness to anticipate potential obstacles that could interfere with your progress

Reviewing the potential pros and cons of making a change as well as the pros and cons of staying the same

Focusing on one small change at a time with clear action steps

Committing to behaving like the person you want to become

WHAT'S NOT HELPFUL

Ignoring or avoiding even thinking about change

Putting off doing anything different until you reach certain milestones or until certain time frames have passed

Allowing your emotions to dictate whether you want to change without considering the logical aspects of doing something different

Making excuses for why you can't do anything different

Only focusing on the negative aspects of change without considering the positive

Convincing yourself not to bother trying to change because you don't think you can do it

Waiting until you feel like creating change

CHAPTER 4

THEY DON'T FOCUS ON THINGS THEY CAN'T CONTROL

You may not control all the events that happen to you, but you can decide not to be reduced by them.
—MAYA ANGELOU

James entered my therapy office because he was upset by his ongoing custody battle. James had struggled with his ex-wife, Carmen, for custody of their seven-year-old daughter for over three years. The judge had given primary custody to Carmen, allowing James visitation on Wednesday evenings and weekends. James was outraged by the judge's decision, as he was certain he was the better parent. James was convinced that Carmen was out to get him and destroy his relationship with his daughter. He'd recently informed Carmen that he was planning a whale-watching excursion for his daughter. When the trip neared, however, his daughter informed him that her mother had taken her whale watching the week prior. James was infuriated. He felt like Carmen was always trying to upstage him or win their daughter's favor by throwing her the biggest birthday parties, buying her the most expensive Christmas gifts, and taking her on the most lavish vacations. James couldn't afford to keep up with his ex-wife financially nor did he want to compete with her lack of discipline. Carmen allowed their daughter to stay up late, play outside alone, and eat as much junk food as she wanted. He tried to talk to Carmen about his concerns many times, but she made it clear she wasn't interested in his opinion. James was pretty sure Carmen just wanted him to look like the bad guy in the eyes of their daughter.

He also didn't like the fact that his ex-wife was dating again because he worried about the type of men their daughter would be exposed to. He even told Carmen that he saw her boyfriend with another woman once, in the hopes that they would break up. His plan backfired when she threatened to get a restraining order against him if he didn't leave her alone.

James initially came to therapy not because he wanted help dealing with his emotions, but because he was looking for a legal ally. He wanted me to write a letter to the court outlining the reasons why he should have full custody of his daughter. When I explained that I couldn't do that, he initially said he didn't think therapy could possibly be helpful. But, instead of leaving, he just kept talking.

When I asked him how effective his previous attempts to change the judge's mind had been, he acknowledged that the judge was pretty clear that the custody order was going to remain in place, whether he liked it or not. He also admitted he hadn't been able to convince Carmen to make any changes, despite his intense efforts. By the end of the session, James actually agreed to come to another appointment.

During his next appointment, we discussed how his attempts to control the situation were negatively affecting his daughter. He recognized how his anger toward his ex-wife interfered with his relationship with his little girl. We discussed some strategies that could help him refocus some of his efforts on improving his relationship with his daughter instead.

By the time James returned for his third and final session I knew he got it when he said, "I should have focused on having fun with my daughter when we went whale watching, rather than spending the entire trip texting angry messages to her mother about how I didn't appreciate her attempts to overshadow me." He also recognized that although he didn't agree with some of Carmen's rules, dragging her back to court repeatedly wasn't likely *to help resolve the situation. Instead, he'd only be wasting more money that he could be spending on their daughter. He decided that he should focus his energy on being the best role model he could be for their daughter, so he could be a positive influence in her life.*

KEEPING EVERYTHING UNDER CONTROL

It feels so safe to have everything under control, but thinking we have the power to always pull the strings can become problematic. Do you respond positively to any of these points below?

❑ You spend a lot of time and energy trying to prevent anything bad from happening.

❑ You invest energy into wishing other people would change.

❑ When faced with a tough situation, you think you can single-handedly fix everything.

❑ You believe the outcome of any situation is entirely based on how much effort you choose to exert.

❑ You assume that good luck has nothing to do with success. Instead, it's completely up to you to determine your future.

❑ Other people sometimes accuse you of being a "control freak."

❑ You struggle to delegate tasks to other people because you don't think they'll do the job right.

❑ Even when you recognize you aren't able to completely control a situation, you struggle to let it go.

❑　If you fail at something, you believe you are solely responsible.

❑　You don't feel comfortable asking for help.

❑　You think people who don't reach their goals are completely responsible for their situation.

❑　You struggle with teamwork because you doubt the abilities of other people on the team.

❑　You have difficulty establishing meaningful relationships because you don't trust people.

Are you guilty of any of the examples above? We can't possibly make all our circumstances and all the people in our lives fit into the way we think things *should* be. When you learn to let go of the details you can't control, the amount of time and energy you'll be able to devote to the things you can control will give you the ability to accomplish incredible feats.

WHY WE TRY TO CONTROL EVERYTHING

James felt very guilty about the divorce. He had tried to make his marriage work with Carmen, because he wanted their daughter to grow up in a stable home. When their relationship ended, he didn't want their daughter to suffer.

Clearly, James was a loving father who worried about his daughter's well-being. It was terrifying for him to recognize how little control he had over what happened to his daughter when she was with her mother. To reduce his anxiety, he tried to control as much of the situation as he could. He thought that if he were able to control everything—from who his ex-wife dated to the type of rules she had in her home—he would feel better.

Trying to control everything usually starts out as a way to manage anxiety. If you know you have everything under control, what's there to worry about? Rather than focusing on managing your anxiety, you try controlling your environment.

The desire to fix everything can also stem from a sort of superhero complex. We hold on to the mistaken belief that if we just try hard enough, everything will turn out the way we want. Rather than delegating a task to a coworker, or trusting a spouse to run an errand, we often choose to do it ourselves to make sure it will be "done right" because we don't trust in other people's capabilities.

LOCUS OF CONTROL

Deciding what is within your control and what isn't depends largely upon your belief system. The psychology field refers to this as your locus of control. People with an external locus of control believe that their lives depend highly on fate, luck, or destiny. They're more likely to believe "Whatever's meant to be will be."

People with an internal locus of control believe they have complete control over their future. They take full responsibility for their successes and failures in life. They believe they have the ability to control everything from their financial future to their health.

Your locus of control will determine how you view your circumstances. Imagine a person who attends a job interview. He possesses the qualifications, education, and experience the company is looking for. But a few days after the interview, he receives a call telling him he didn't get the job. If he has an external locus of control he'll think, *They probably had some overquali-*

fied people apply for the position. It wasn't the right job for me anyway. If he has an internal locus of control, he's more likely to think, *I must not have done a good job impressing them. I knew I should have redone my résumé. I've also got to sharpen my interview skills.*

Several factors influence your locus of control. Your childhood experiences certainly play a role. If you grew up in a family where hard work was valued, you may lean more toward an internal locus of control, because you'll believe that hard work can pay off. If however, you grew up with parents who drilled into you things such as, "Your vote doesn't matter in this world," or "No matter what you do, the world will always keep you down," you may have developed an external locus of control.

Your experiences throughout life can also influence your locus of control. If you achieve success when you try hard, you'll see that you have a lot of control over the outcome. But if you feel like no matter what you do, things just don't turn out right, you may begin to feel like you have less control.

An internal locus of control has often been idealized as the "best" way to be. Ideas like "You can do anything if you just put your mind to it" have been valued in many cultures. In fact, people with a high sense of control often make great CEOs because they believe in their ability to make a difference. Doctors like having patients with a strong internal locus of control because they do everything possible to treat and prevent illness. But there are also potential downsides to believing you can control *everything.*

THE PROBLEM WITH WASTING ENERGY ON THINGS YOU CAN'T CONTROL

James wasted a lot of time, energy, and money on trying to change his custody situation even though his repeated court appearances clearly weren't influencing the judge's decision. Although he initially thought that exerting more effort into controlling the situation would reduce his stress, over the long term, his stress increased each time he failed at his attempts to gain more control. His attempts to gain control also negatively impacted his relationship with his daughter. Instead of enjoying their time together and focusing on nurturing their relationship, he grilled her with questions to learn more about what was going on at her mother's house. There are several problems associated with trying to control everything:

- *Trying to maintain complete control leads to increased anxiety.* Efforts to manage your anxiety by trying to control everything in your environment will backfire. The more unsuccessful your attempts to control the situation are, the more anxious you'll become. It can lead to feelings of inadequacy as you see that you aren't able to fully control the outcome.

- *Attempting to control everything wastes time and energy.* Worrying about things outside of your control wastes mental energy. Wishing circumstances were different, trying to convince people they have to do everything your way, and attempting to prevent anything bad from ever happening is exhausting. It takes energy away from actively problem solving and the issues you do have control over.

- *Being a control freak damages relationships.* Telling people what they should do or how to do things right isn't likely to attract many friends. In fact, many who have control issues struggle to get close to people because they don't trust others with any type of responsibility.

- *You'll judge others harshly.* If you credit all your success in life to your abilities, you'll criticize people who haven't achieved the same. In fact, people with a high internal locus of control tend to suffer from loneliness because they feel irritable that other people aren't keeping up with their standards.

- *You'll unnecessarily blame yourself for everything.* You can't prevent bad things from happening all the time. But, if you think everything is within your control, you'll believe you're directly responsible every time life doesn't go according to your plan.

DEVELOP A BALANCED SENSE OF CONTROL

James couldn't move forward until he accepted that he didn't have complete control over the custody situation. Once he was able to recognize this, he could focus on the things he did have control over—like improving his relationship with his daughter. He also wanted to focus on establishing at least a civil relationship with his ex-wife, but to do that, he needed to continue reminding himself that he couldn't control what went on in her home. Clearly, if he recognized any signs that his daughter was being seriously harmed, he could act, but eating ice cream and staying up late didn't rise to the level of danger that would make a judge give him custody.

Those who strike the right balance of control recognize how their behaviors can affect their chances of success, but they also identify how external factors, such as being in the right place at the right time, can play a role. Researchers found that these people have a bi-locus of control, as opposed to a complete internal or external locus of control. To achieve this balance in your own life, be willing to examine your beliefs about what you truly can control and what you can't. Take notice of times when you've devoted too much energy to people and circumstances that you just couldn't change. Remind yourself that there's a lot you can't control:

- You can host a good party, but you can't control whether people have fun.

- You can give your child tools to be successful, but you can't make your child be a good student.

- You can do your best at your job, but you can't force your boss to recognize your work.

- You can sell a great product, but you can't dictate who buys it.

- You may be the smartest person in the room, but you can't control whether people choose to follow your advice.

- You can nag, beg, and make threats, but you can't force your spouse to behave differently.

- You can have the most positive attitude in the world, but it can't make a terminal diagnosis disappear.

- You can control how much you take care of yourself, but you can't always prevent illness.

- You can control what you're doing, but you can't control your competitor.

IDENTIFY YOUR FEARS

In 2005, Heather Von St. James was diagnosed with mesothelioma when her daughter was just three months old. As a little girl, she had worn her father's construction jacket for fun. His jacket had most likely been exposed to asbestos, which has been linked to mesothelioma and could explain why at only thirty-six, Heather had what is known as an "old man's disease."

Doctors initially gave Heather fifteen months to live. With radiation and chemotherapy, they said she might live up to five years. She was, however, a prime candidate for lung removal, and although the surgery was risky, it was her best chance for survival.

Heather chose to undergo the extensive surgery that would remove the affected lung and the lining around her lung as well as replace half of her diaphragm and the lining of her heart with surgical Gore-Tex. She remained hospitalized for a month following the operation. When she was discharged from the hospital, she went to stay with her parents for a few months so they could help her care for her baby while her husband returned to work. When Heather returned home three months later, she underwent radiation and chemotherapy. It took her almost a year to begin feeling better again, but to this day, she remains cancer free. Although she becomes out of breath more easily with physical exertion now that she only has one lung, she considers it a relatively small price to pay.

To commemorate the anniversary of the day she got her lung removed, Heather now celebrates, "Lung Leavin' Day" on February 2 each year. Each year on "Lung Leavin' Day," Heather acknowledges her fears about the things she doesn't have control over—like the possibility of the cancer returning. She uses a marker to write those fears on a plate and then she symbolically lets go of those fears by smashing the plate into a fire. Within just a few short years, the celebration has grown. Today, more than eighty friends and family attend. Guests join in by writing down their own fears and smashing their plates into the fire. They've even turned it into a fund-raiser for mesothelioma research.

"Cancer leaves you feeling so out of control," Heather acknowledges. Although she is currently cancer free, she admits that she continues to be fearful that her daughter may have to grow up without a mother. But she chooses to face her fears head-on by writing down what scares her most, and recognizing that those things are not within her control. She then chooses to focus her efforts on what she does have control over—like living every day to the fullest.

Heather now works as a patient advocate for mesothelioma. She speaks with newly diagnosed patients and helps them deal with their fears about cancer. She's also a keynote speaker who delivers her message of hope and healing.

When you notice yourself trying to control something that you can't, ask yourself, *What am I so afraid of?* Do you worry someone else is going to make a bad choice? Do you worry that something is going to go terribly wrong? Are you terrified that you won't be successful? Acknowledging your fears, and developing an understanding of them, will help you begin to recognize what is within your control and what isn't.

FOCUS ON WHAT YOU CAN CONTROL

Once you've identified your fears, identify what you can control, bearing in mind that sometimes the only thing you can control is your behavior and attitude.

You can't control what happens to your luggage once you hand it to an airline employee at the airport. But what you can control is what you pack in your carry-on bag. If you have your most important belongings and an extra change of clothing with you, it won't feel like such an emergency if your luggage doesn't arrive at your destination on time. By focusing on what you can control, it is much easier to let go of worrying about what you can't.

When you notice you have a lot of anxiety about a situation, do what you can to manage your reaction and influence the outcome. But recognize that you can't control other people, and you can't ever have complete control over the end result.

INFLUENCE PEOPLE WITHOUT TRYING TO CONTROL THEM

Jenny was twenty years old when she chose to drop out of college. After spending a couple of years working toward a degree in education, she decided she didn't really want to be a math teacher. To her mother's horror, she wanted to pursue art instead.

Every day Jenny's mother called to tell Jenny she was ruining her life. She made it clear she would never support Jenny's choice to drop out of school. She even threatened to cut off contact with Jenny if she didn't choose to take "the right path."

Jenny quickly got sick of her mother's daily criticisms over her choices. She told her mother several times that she was not going back to college and her insults and threats wouldn't change her mind. But her mother persisted because she worried about what type of future Jenny would have as an artist.

Eventually, Jenny stopped answering the phone. She stopped going to her mother's house for dinner, too. After all, it wasn't enjoyable to hear her mother lecture her about how college dropouts and aspiring artists don't ever make it in the real world. Even though Jenny was a grown adult, her mother wanted to control what she did. It was painful for her to sit on the sidelines and watch Jenny make choices she felt were irresponsible. She imagined her daughter would always be broke, unhappy, and struggling just to survive. Jenny's mother mistakenly believed she could control what Jenny did with her life. Unfortunately, her attempts to control Jenny ruined their relationship without motivating Jenny to do anything different.

It's hard to sit back and watch other people engage in behavior we don't approve of, especially if that behavior is something we view as self-destructive. But making demands, nagging, and begging won't yield the results you want. Here are strategies to influence others without trying to force them to change:

- *Listen first, speak second.* Other people are often less defensive when they feel like you've taken the time to hear what they have to say.

- *Share your opinion and concerns, but only share it once.* Repeating your unease over and over again won't make your words any more effective. In fact, it can backfire.

- *Change your behavior.* If a wife doesn't want her husband to drink, emptying his beer cans down the drain isn't going to motivate him to stop drinking. But she can choose to spend time with him when he's sober and not be around him when he's drinking. If he enjoys spending time with her, he may choose to remain sober more often.

- *Point out the positive.* If someone is making a genuine effort to create change, whether it's to stop smoking or start exercising, offer some genuine praise. Just don't go overboard or say something like, "See, I told you that you'd feel better if you quit eating all that junk food." Backhanded compliments or an "I told you so" don't motivate people to change.

PRACTICE ACCEPTANCE

Imagine a man stuck in a traffic jam. Traffic hasn't moved an inch for twenty minutes and he's running late for a meeting. He starts yelling, swearing, and banging his fists on the steering wheel. He wants so much to be in control that he just can't tolerate the fact that he's going to be late. *These people should just get out of my way,* he thinks. *It's ridiculous that there's this much traffic in the middle of the afternoon.*

Contrast that person with someone in the car next to him who turns on the radio and chooses to sing along to some of his favorite tunes while he waits. He figures, *I'll get there when I can.* He uses his time and energy wisely because he knows he has no control over when traffic will start moving again. Instead, he tells himself, *There are millions of cars on the road every day. Sometimes traffic jams are bound to happen.*

Either of these people could choose to do something different in the future to avoid traffic. They could leave earlier, take a different route, use public transportation, check the traffic report ahead of time, or even start a movement to try and change the road systems. But, for now, they have the choice to accept that they're stuck in a traffic jam or focus on the fact that they feel an injustice is being done.

Even though you might not like the situation you're in, you can choose to accept it. You can accept that your boss is mean, that your mother doesn't approve of you, or that your kids aren't striving to be high achievers. That doesn't mean you can't work toward influencing them by changing your behavior, but it does mean you can stop trying to force them to be different.

GIVING UP CONTROL
WILL MAKE YOU STRONGER

At the age of eighteen, Terry Fox was diagnosed with osteosarcoma. Doctors amputated his leg but warned him that his survival rate was only 50 percent. They also made it clear that major advances had been made in cancer treatment over the past few years. Just two years previously, the survival rate for this type of cancer was only 15 percent.

Within three weeks of his surgery, Fox was walking with the help of a prosthetic limb. His doctors noted that his positive attitude most likely had something to do with his rapid recovery. He underwent sixteen months of chemotherapy and during that time, he met many other patients who were dying from cancer. By the time his treatment ended, he decided to spread the word about the need for more funding for cancer research.

On the night before he got his leg amputated, he'd read a story about a man who had run the New York City marathon with a prosthetic leg. The article inspired him to begin running as soon as he was physically able. He ran his first marathon in British Columbia, and though he finished in last place, he was met with a lot of support at the finish line.

After completing the marathon, Fox hatched a fund-raising plan. He decided to run across Canada by completing a marathon every single day. Initially, he hoped to earn a million dollars for charity, but he soon set his sights even higher. He wanted to raise one dollar for each person in Canada—a grand total of $24 million.

In April of 1980, he set out to run over twenty-six miles a day. As word of his trek began to spread, his support increased. Communities began holding large receptions to commemorate his arrival in their town. He was asked to give speeches, and the amount of money he raised increased.

Fox ran for an amazing 143 days straight. But his run came to an end one day when he couldn't catch his breath and he began experiencing chest pain. He was taken to the hospital and doctors confirmed that his cancer had returned and spread to his lungs. After running over three thousand miles, he was forced to stop.

His journey had raised over $1.7 million by the time he was hospitalized. But as the news of his hospitalization circulated, he gained even more support. A five-hour telethon raised $10.5 million. Donations continued and by the next spring, Fox had raised over $23 million. Although he attempted a variety of treatments, his cancer continued to spread, and in June of 1981, Fox died from complications of his cancer.

Fox understood he couldn't control every aspect of his health. He couldn't stop people from getting cancer. He couldn't even control the spread of the disease in his own body. Instead of focusing on those things, he chose to put his energy into the things he could control.

In his letter requesting support prior to his run, Fox made it clear he didn't think his run would cure cancer, but he knew it would make a difference. "The running thing I can do, even if I have to crawl every last mile," he said.

His choice to do something that seemed unimaginable gave him a purpose that continues today. Each year, countries all over the world participate in the Terry Fox run. Over $650 million has been raised in his honor.

When you stop trying to control every aspect of your life, you'll have more time and energy to devote to things you can control. Here are some of the benefits you'll experience:

- **Increased happiness**—The maximum level of happiness is achieved when people have a balanced locus of control. Coined as a "bi-local expectancy," the people who understand that they can take a lot of steps to control their lives while also recognizing the limitations of their ability are happier than people who think they can control everything.

- **Better relationships**—When you give up your need for control, you'll likely experience better relationships. You'll have fewer trust issues and you'll welcome more people into your life. You may be more willing to ask for help, and other people are likely to view you as less critical. Research indicates that people who stop trying to control everything experience an increased sense of belonging and community.

- **Less stress**—When you stop carrying around the weight of the world, you'll feel less stressed. You may experience more short-term anxiety as you give up control, but over the long term, you'll have a lot less stress and anxiety.

- **New opportunities**—When you have a strong need to control things, you'll be less likely to invite change into your life because there aren't any guarantees of a positive outcome. When you choose to give up your need to control everything, you'll have increased confidence in your ability to handle new opportunities.

- **More success**—Although most people who want to control everything have a deep desire to be successful, having an internal locus of control can actually interfere with your chances of success. Research shows that it's possible to become so focused on ensuring you'll be successful, you could actually overlook opportunities that could help you advance. When you give up your desire to control everything, you'll be more willing to look around and you may recognize good fortune that comes your way even if it isn't directly related to your behavior.

TROUBLESHOOTING AND COMMON TRAPS

When you focus on what's wrong with the world, without looking at how you can control your attitude and behavior, you'll find yourself stuck. Instead of wasting energy trying to prevent a storm, focus on how you can prepare for it.

WHAT'S HELPFUL

Delegating tasks and responsibilities to other people

Asking for help when you need it

Focusing on solving problems that are within your control

Keeping the emphasis on influencing others rather than controlling them

Thinking balanced thoughts about what is within your control and what isn't

Not relying on yourself for the entire outcome

WHAT'S NOT HELPFUL

Insisting on doing everything because no one else can do it right

Choosing to do everything on your own because you think you should be able to accomplish things without help

Spending time trying to figure out how to change things that are likely beyond your direct control

Trying to force other people to do what you think they should do, regardless of how they feel

Only thinking about what you can do to make things turn out the way you want

Taking full responsibility for the end result without acknowledging other factors that influence the outcome

CHAPTER 5

THEY DON'T WORRY ABOUT PLEASING EVERYONE

Care about what other people think and you will
always be their prisoner.
—LAO TZU

Megan entered my therapy office looking for help because she was feeling stressed out and overwhelmed. She said there weren't enough hours in the day to accomplish everything she needed to do.

At age thirty-five, she was married and had two young children. She worked a part-time job, taught Sunday school, and was the Girl Scout troop leader. She strived to be a good wife and mother, but she felt like she just wasn't doing a good enough job. She was often irritable and grumpy toward her family and she wasn't sure why.

The more Megan talked, the clearer it became that she was a woman who couldn't say no. Church members frequently called her on Saturday nights, asking her to bake muffins for Sunday morning's church service. Parents of her Girl Scout troop sometimes relied on her to drive their children home if they were stuck at work.

Megan also frequently babysat for her sister's kids, so her sister wouldn't have to spend money on a sitter. She also had a cousin who sought favors and always seemed to have some sort of last-minute problem, ranging from being short on cash to needing help with a home improvement project. Lately, Megan had stopped answering her cousin's phone calls because she knew that every time she called she needed something.

Megan said to me that her number one rule was to never say no to family. So each time her cousin asked for a favor or her sister asked her to babysit, she automatically said yes. When I asked her what impact that had on her husband and children, she told me that sometimes it meant she wasn't home in time for dinner or to put the kids to bed. Just admitting that out loud helped Megan begin to realize why saying yes to extended family meant she was saying no to her immediate family. Although she valued her extended family, her husband and her children were her top priorities, and she decided she needed to start treating them accordingly.

We also reviewed her desire to be liked by everyone. Her biggest fear was that other people would think she was selfish. However, after a few therapy sessions she began to recognize that her need to always be liked was actually much more selfish than saying no to someone. Helping others really wasn't about improving their lives; she was mostly giving of herself because she wanted to be held in higher regard. Once she changed the way she thought about people pleasing, she was able to begin changing her behavior.

It took some practice for Megan to begin saying no to people. In fact, she wasn't even sure how to say no. She thought she needed an excuse but she didn't want to lie. But I encouraged her to simply say something like "No, I'm not able to do that," without providing a lengthy reason why. She began practicing saying no and she found that the more she did it, the easier it became. Although she had imagined people would become angry with her, she quickly noticed that they didn't really seem to mind. The more time she spent with her family, the less irritable she felt. Her stress level also decreased and after saying no a few times, she felt less pressured to please others.

PEOPLE-PLEASING SIGNS

While in chapter 2 we discussed how giving away your power is about allowing people to control how you feel; people pleasing is about trying to control how other people feel. Do you respond positively to any of the points below?

- ❏ You feel responsible for how other people feel.

- ❏ The thought of anyone being mad at you causes you to feel uncomfortable.

- ❏ You tend to be a "pushover."

- ❏ You find it easier to agree with people rather than express a contrary opinion.

- ❏ You often apologize even when you don't think you did anything wrong.

- ❏ You go to great lengths to avoid conflict.

- ❏ You don't usually tell people when you're feeling offended or your feelings are hurt.

- ❏ You tend to say yes when people ask you for favors, even if you really don't want to do something.

- ❏ You change your behavior based on what you think other people want.

- ❏ You put a lot of energy into trying to impress people.

- ❏ If you hosted a party and people didn't seem to be enjoying themselves, you'd feel responsible.

❑ You seek praise and approval from people in your life often.

❑ When someone around you is upset, you take responsibility for trying to make him or her feel better.

❑ You would never want anyone to think you are selfish.

❑ You often feel overscheduled and overburdened by all the things you have to do.

Do any of those examples sound familiar? Attempts to be a "nice person" can backfire when your behavior crosses over into people pleasing. It can take a serious toll on all areas of your life and make it impossible to reach your goals. You can still be a kind and generous person without trying to please everyone.

WHY WE TRY TO PLEASE PEOPLE

Megan strived to develop a reputation as someone who could always meet other people's needs. Her self-worth was fueled by the way other people seemed to perceive her. She went to such great lengths to make others happy because in her mind the alternatives—finding herself in the midst of conflict, feeling rejected, or losing relationships—were much worse than the emotional and physical exhaustion she felt.

FEAR

Conflict and confrontation can be uncomfortable. It's usually not enjoyable to sit between squabbling coworkers in a meeting. And who wants to attend a family holiday gathering when their relatives are arguing? Fearing conflict, we tell ourselves, *If I can make everyone happy, everything will be okay.*

When a people pleaser sees a car approaching quickly, he may drive faster because he thinks, *That guy is in a hurry. I don't want to make him mad by going too slow.* People pleasers may also fear rejection or abandonment. *If I don't make you happy, you won't like me.* They thrive on praise and reassurance from others, and if they're not receiving enough positive reinforcement, they change their behavior to try and make people feel happy.

LEARNED BEHAVIOR

Sometimes the desire to avoid conflict stems from childhood. If you were raised by parents who were constantly bickering, you may have learned that conflict is bad and keeping people happy is the best way to prevent arguments.

Children of alcoholics, for example, often grow up to be people pleasers because that was the best way to deal with a parent's unpredictable behavior. In other cases, doing good deeds was the only way to get any attention.

Putting other people first can also become a way to feel needed and important. *I'm worth something if I can make other people feel happy.* So it becomes a habit to always invest energy into other people's feelings and lives.

A lot of my clients will often tell me they need to behave like a doormat, because that's what the Bible says they should do. But I'm pretty sure the Bible says to "treat your neighbor as yourself," not better than yourself. Most spiritual guidance encourages us to be bold enough to live according to our values, even when doing so displeases some people.

THE PROBLEM WITH PEOPLE PLEASING

Megan's desire to please others made her lose sight of her values. She wasn't getting her needs met and it impacted her mood. She realized exactly how much her increased attempts to please others had affected her family when—after a few therapy sessions—her husband said to her, "I feel like I've got my old Megan back."

YOUR ASSUMPTIONS AREN'T ALWAYS TRUE

Sally invites Jane to go shopping with her. The only reason Sally invites Jane is because Jane asked her out for coffee last week and Sally thinks it would be nice to reciprocate. However, Sally actually hopes Jane declines because she wants to make it a quick trip to the mall to pick out some shoes. She knows if Jane goes, she'll likely want to shop for hours.

Jane actually doesn't want to go shopping. She has some errands to run and a few household chores to finish up. But she doesn't want to hurt Sally's feelings. So when Sally invites her to the mall, she agrees to go.

Both of these women think they're doing something that pleases the other person. However, they clearly have no idea what the other person wants. Their "attempts to be nice" are actually causing more of a nuisance to each other. But neither one has the courage to actually speak up and say what she really wants.

Most of us wrongly assume that people-pleasing behavior proves we're generous. But when you think about it, always trying to please people isn't a selfless act. It's actually quite self-centered. It assumes that everyone cares about your every move. It also assumes you think you have the power to control how other people feel.

If you're constantly doing things to make others happy and you don't think they are appreciative of your efforts, you'll soon experience resentment. Thoughts such as *I do so much for you, but you don't do anything for me* will creep in and ultimately hurt your relationships.

PEOPLE PLEASING DAMAGES RELATIONSHIPS

Angela didn't try to please everyone in her life, just the men she dated. If she was on a date with a man who said he liked women with a sense of humor, she'd make a few extra jokes. If she was on a date with a man who said he liked spontaneous women, she'd tell him all about the last-minute trip to France she took last summer. If, however, another man said he liked smart women, she'd talk about that same trip to France but this time she'd say she went because she wanted to view fine art.

Angela did whatever she could to try to make herself appear more attractive to whomever she was dating. She felt that if she said enough things that were pleasing to her date, she'd get to go on a second date. She didn't think about the long-term consequences of her ever-changing personality. Eventually, she wasn't able to please anyone quite enough to stay with her for the long haul.

No respectable man wanted to date a shell of a woman who behaved like a puppet. In fact, a lot of her dates got annoyed fairly quickly by Angela because she constantly agreed with everything they said. Her attempts to say whatever they wanted to hear were usually pretty transparent.

Angela feared that if she disagreed with a date or held an opposing opinion, he would no longer be interested in her, which reveals her lack of trust. *You won't keep me around unless I do what you want,* she thought. If you truly care about someone and you believe the person cares about you, you'd have to be willing to tell that individual the truth. You recognize that even if that person doesn't like something you say or do, he or she can still enjoy your company.

It's an impossible feat to always make everyone around you happy. Perhaps your father-in-law asks you to help him on a project. But if you leave to go help him, your spouse will get angry because you had already made plans to have lunch together. When faced with such a decision, people pleasers will often choose to risk not pleasing the person closest to them. They know that their spouse will eventually get over being offended. Unfortunately, this leaves the people you love the most feeling hurt or angry. Shouldn't we do the opposite? Shouldn't we work the hardest on the most intimate and special relationships?

Ever met someone who behaves like a martyr? Such individuals' attempts to please others actually becomes a turnoff. They're constantly saying things like "I do everything around here" or "If I don't do it, no one will." Martyrs risk becoming angry, bitter people, as their attempts to make others happy backfire.

Whether you're guilty of thinking you're a martyr, or you simply struggle to say no when you fear you'll hurt someone's feelings, there aren't any guarantees people will like you just because you try to please them. Instead, they may simply start taking advantage of you without forming a deeper relationship based on trust and mutual respect.

PEOPLE PLEASERS LOSE SIGHT OF THEIR VALUES

Bronnie Ware, an Australian nurse who spent many years working with patients who were dying, cites people pleasing as one of the biggest regrets she heard her patients share on their deathbeds. In her book, *The Top Five Regrets of the Dying,* she explains how dying people often said they wished they had lived a more authentic life. Instead of dressing, acting, and speaking in a manner that was pleasing to others, they'd wished they'd been true to themselves.

There's even research published in the *Journal of Social and Clinical Psychology* that shows people pleasers in a study tended to eat more when they thought it would make others around them happier. They were willing to sabotage their own health if they thought it would help the other people in the room even though they had no evidence that the people around them were even paying attention to what they were eating.

Pleasing people will hold you back from reaching your full potential. Although people pleasers want to be liked, they often don't want to be the best at anything because they fear being held in too high regard could make other people feel bad. Someone may not get that promotion at work because he doesn't feel comfortable taking credit for the work he's done. Or a woman who gets approached by an attractive man may choose not to reciprocate friendly conversation because she doesn't want to make her friend feel bad that he didn't start talking to her first.

No matter what your values are, you'll stop behaving according to them if you're focused primarily on pleasing other people. You'll quickly lose sight of doing what's right and try only to do what makes other people happy. Just because it's a popular choice doesn't mean it's the right choice.

AVOID PEOPLE PLEASING

Saying yes had become such a habit for Megan that she found herself agreeing to do things automatically.

So I helped her to develop a mantra where she repeated to herself, "Saying yes to others means saying no to my husband and kids." She knew it was okay to say yes to some things without her husband and children being negatively affected. She just couldn't say yes all the time or her mood and family would suffer.

DETERMINE WHO YOU WANT TO PLEASE

If you want to be successful at reaching your goals, you need to define your path, not just do what other people want you to do. Craigslist CEO Jim Buckmaster knows the importance of this firsthand.

Buckmaster became the CEO of Craigslist in 2000. While other websites were capitalizing on advertising, Craigslist wasn't. In fact, Craigslist turned down a variety of revenue-generating opportunities. Instead, Buckmaster and the team decided to keep the website simple, and only charge users for a very few specific types of listings. The bulk of user-generated listings has remained a free service. In fact, the company doesn't even have a marketing team.

Craigslist received a lot of backlash for this decision and Buckmaster has been the target of much criticism. He's been accused of being anticapitalistic and even called a "social anarchist." But Buckmaster didn't try to please his critics. Instead, he continued running Craigslist the way it has always operated.

His willingness to go against the grain and prevent Craigslist from depending too heavily on advertisements has likely kept the business running. It survived the dot-com crash with ease and continues to be one of the most popular websites in the world. Craigslist has been estimated to be worth at least $5 billion. By not worrying about trying to please everyone, Buckmaster was able to keep the company focused on serving its purpose and reaching its audience.

Before you automatically change your behavior based on what you think other people want, evaluate your thoughts and feelings. When you second-guess whether you should express your opinion, remember these truths about people pleasing:

- *Worrying about trying to please everyone is a waste of time.* You can't control how other people feel and the more time you spend devoting your thoughts to wondering if people will be happy, the less time you'll have to think about what really matters.

- *People pleasers are easily manipulated.* Others can recognize a people pleaser a mile away. Manipulators often use tactics to prey on people pleasers' emotions and control their behavior. Be on the lookout for people who say things like "I'm only asking you to do to this because you'd do the best job" or "I hate to ask you this, but . . ."

- *It's okay for other people to feel angry or disappointed.* There is no reason that people need to feel happy or pleased all the time. Everyone has the ability to cope with a wide array of feelings, and it's not your job to prevent them from feeling negative emotions. Just because someone gets mad, it doesn't necessarily mean you did anything wrong.

- *You can't please everyone.* It's impossible for everyone to be delighted by the same things. Accept that some people will just never be pleased, and it isn't your job to make them happy.

CLARIFY YOUR VALUES

Imagine a single mother who works a full-time job at a factory. One day, when she wakes her son up for school, he says he doesn't feel well. She checks his temperature and he has a slight fever. Clearly, he can't go to school.

She has to decide what to do with him for the day. She doesn't have any friends or family members who can stay with him. She could call in sick to her job, but she won't get paid if she takes the day off. If she doesn't get paid for the day, she'll struggle to afford groceries for the week. She also worries that missing another day of work could put her job at risk. She's already missed a lot of days due to the children being sick.

She decides to leave her son home alone for the day. She knows other people will likely have a negative opinion about her choice to leave a sick child home alone when he's only ten years old. However, her values tell her it's the right choice given her circumstances, regardless of how others may judge her. It's not that she values her job more than her son. In fact, she values her family more than anything. But she knows that going to work is best for the greater good of her family in the long run.

When you're faced with decisions in your life, it's important to know exactly what your values are so you can make the best choices. Could you easily list your top five values off the top of your head? Most people can't. But if you aren't really clear on your values, how do you know where to put your energy, and how to make the best decisions? Taking time to clarify your values can be a very worthwhile exercise. Common values include:

- Children

- Romantic relationship

- Extended family

- Religious/Spiritual beliefs

- Volunteering or helping other people

- Career

- Money

- Maintaining good friendships

- Taking care of your physical health

- Having a sense of purpose

- Leisure activities

- Pleasing people

- Education

Pick your top five values in life and rank them in order from most important to least important. Now stop and think about whether you are actually living according to those values. How much of your time, money, energy, and skill is devoted to each one? Are you putting too much effort into something that's not even on your list?

Where on your list does pleasing people fall? It should never be at the top. Reviewing the order of your list from time to time can help you determine if your life is out of balance.

TAKE TIME TO DECIDE WHETHER TO SAY YES OR NO

In the case of Megan, she avoided her cousin because she knew she couldn't say no if she was asked to do a favor. To help her say no, we developed a script. Whenever anyone asked her to do something, she responded by saying, "Let me see what I have going on and I'll get back to you." That bought her some time to really think about whether she wanted to do something. Then, she could ensure that if she said yes it was because she wanted to, not simply because she wanted to please others at her own expense.

If automatically saying yes has become a habit in your life, learn how to evaluate your decision before giving an answer.

When someone asks you to do something, ask yourself these questions before responding:

- *Is this something I want to do?* Most people pleasers don't even know what they want because they're so used to doing things automatically. Take a moment to evaluate your opinion.

- *What will I have to give up by doing this?* If you do something for someone else, you'll have to give something up. Maybe it's time with your family or perhaps it will cost you money. Before making a decision, recognize what saying yes will mean for you.

- *What will I gain by doing this?* Maybe it will give you an opportunity to improve your relationship, or maybe doing something like this will likely be something you enjoy. Think about the potential benefits of saying yes.

- *How will I feel if I do it?* Are you likely to feel angry and resentful? Or will you feel happy and proud? Take some time to imagine how you're likely to feel as you weigh your options.

Like Megan discovered, you don't need to have an excuse about why you can't do something. When you say no, you can say something such as "I wish I could but I'm not going to be able to do that" or "Sorry, but I won't be able to." If you're not used to saying no, it can take some practice, but it gets easier with time.

PRACTICE BEHAVING ASSERTIVELY

Confrontation doesn't have to be bad or scary. In fact, assertive discussions can actually be quite healthy and sharing your concerns can improve relationships. At one point, Megan confronted her cousin and told her that she felt like she had been taken advantage of in the past. Her cousin apologized, said she had no idea Megan ever felt like that and she wanted to make sure it wouldn't happen again. Megan accepted some responsibility for her feelings and her behavior, since she didn't speak up to say no when she was asked to do things she didn't want to do. Megan and her cousin were able to repair their relationship instead of allowing it to dissolve.

Speak up if someone takes advantage of you and ask for what you need. You don't have to be demanding or rude, but instead, remain respectful and polite. Express your feelings and stick to the facts. Use "I" statements, such as "I'm frustrated that you're always thirty minutes late," instead of "You're never on time."

I work with a lot of parents who can't stand it when their children aren't happy. They don't want to tell their kids they can't do something because they don't want their kids to cry or accuse them of being mean. Whether it's your children, a friend, a co-worker, or even a stranger, sometimes it feels uncomfortable to know someone is angry at you if you're not used to speaking up for yourself. But with practice, that discomfort becomes easier to tolerate and behaving assertively is easier to do.

ACCEPTING THAT YOU CAN'T PLEASE EVERYONE MAKES YOU STRONGER

Mose Gingerich struggled with a decision that most of us can't imagine ever having to make. He was raised in an Amish community in Wisconsin where his days were spent plowing the fields and milking the cows by hand. But Mose wasn't convinced he wanted to remain Amish. In a community where questions were discouraged, Mose questioned everything he'd been taught about God and the Amish way of life.

He spent years wrestling with the idea of leaving the Amish community. The Amish way of life was all he'd ever known. To permanently leave, he'd never again be allowed contact with anyone in the Amish community, including his mother and his siblings. Besides, stepping into the "English world" would be like entering a foreign land. Mose had never been allowed to use modern-day conveniences, like computers, or even electricity. How could he possibly make it on his own in the outside world that he didn't know much about?

Entering a relatively unknown world wasn't the scariest part for Mose. Instead, he was most terrified that he'd go to hell. He'd always been warned that the Amish God was the only God, and to leave the Amish meant he'd be leaving God. The Amish elders told him that there was no hope for people in the outside world. Individuals who left the Amish, but tried to remain Christians, were only playing with fire.

Mose temporarily left his Amish community a couple of times during his teenage and young adult years. He traveled around the country and learned about other Amish cultures and got a taste of the outside world. His explorations helped him to develop his own view of the world and of God. And ultimately, he decided his views weren't in line with the Amish community's beliefs. So Mose decided to leave his Amish life behind once and for all.

Mose created a new life for himself in Missouri, where he's experienced a variety of adventures ranging from opening his own construction business to starring in reality TV shows. He's had to make his own way without any help from his family, because they, and all the other people in his former community, no longer speak to him. Mose sometimes mentors other ex-Amish young people as they struggle to integrate into the "English world" since Mose knows firsthand that finding a job, getting a driver's license, and developing an understanding of cultural norms can be difficult without support.

I had an opportunity to ask him how he made that decision and he told me that by confronting his own beliefs, he realized that "this world is what one makes of it, and that one makes what one chooses. And that those choices were mine. So I chose to leave, and I threw my lot in with the modern world. And every day that I wake up next to my wife, my two girls, and my stepson, I thank God that I did."

If Mose had focused on trying to please everyone, he'd still be living in the Amish community, even though he knew it wasn't right for him. But Mose was strong enough to step away from everything he'd ever been taught, and everyone he'd ever known, to do what he felt was the right choice for him. He's satisfied with the life that he's built for himself, and he's secure enough in who he is to tolerate the disapproval from the entire Amish community.

Your words and your behavior must be in line with your beliefs before you can begin to enjoy a truly authentic life. When you stop worrying about pleasing everyone and, instead, are willing to be bold enough to live according to your own values, you'll experience many benefits:

- *Your self-confidence will soar.* The more you're able to see that you don't have to make people happy, the more independence and confidence you'll gain. You'll feel content with the decisions you make, even when other people disagree with your actions, because you'll know you made the right choice.

- *You'll have more time and energy to devote to your goals.* Instead of wasting energy trying to become the person you think others want you to be, you'll have time and energy to work on yourself. When you channel that effort toward your goals, you'll be much more likely to be successful.

- *You'll feel less stressed.* When you set limits and healthy boundaries, you'll experience a lot less stress and irritation. You'll feel like you have more control over your life.

- *You'll establish healthier relationships.* Other people will develop more respect for you when you behave in an assertive manner. Your communication will improve and you'll be able to prevent yourself from building a lot of anger and resentment toward people.

- *You'll have increased willpower.* An interesting 2008 study published in the *Journal of Experimental Psychology* showed that people have much more willpower when they're making choices on their own accord rather than out of an attempt to please someone else. If you're only doing something to make someone else happy, you'll struggle to reach your goal. You'll be motivated to keep up the good work if you're convinced it's the best choice for you.

TROUBLESHOOTING AND COMMON TRAPS

There may be certain areas of your life where it's easy to behave according to your values, and there may be other areas where you find yourself worrying about pleasing people. Be aware of the warning signs and work on trying to live a life that lines up with your beliefs, not one that will make the most people happy.

WHAT'S HELPFUL

Identifying your values and behaving according to them

Being aware of your emotions before deciding whether to say yes to someone's request

Saying no when you don't want to do something

Practicing tolerating uncomfortable emotions associated with conflict and confrontation

Behaving assertively even when speaking up may not be well received

WHAT'S NOT HELPFUL

Losing sight of who you are and what your values are

Only considering someone else's feelings without thinking about your emotions

Automatically accepting an invitation without considering whether it's a good choice

Agreeing with people and complying with requests to avoid confrontation

Going along with the crowd or refusing to express any opinions that may go against what the majority of people think

CHAPTER 6

THEY DON'T FEAR TAKING CALCULATED RISKS

*Don't be too timid and squeamish about your actions. All life
is an experiment. The more experiments you make the better.*
—RALPH WALDO EMERSON

*Dale had worked as a high school shop teacher for almost thirty years and
although he liked his job, he just wasn't all that passionate about it anymore. He dreamed about the flexibility, freedom, and money he could gain
from opening his own furniture store. But when he'd shared that idea with
his wife, she'd rolled her eyes and referred to him as a dreamer.*

*The more Dale thought about it, the more he believed his wife was
probably right. But he didn't want to keep teaching shop class. Partially
because he was bored with teaching and partially because he knew he was
burned out. He felt like he wasn't as effective at teaching as he used to be.
He didn't think it was fair to his students for him to keep teaching indefinitely.*

*The dream of opening his own business certainly wasn't the first
big idea Dale had ever had. He'd once dreamed of living on a sailboat.
During another phase of his life, he'd wanted to open a bed-and-breakfast
in Hawaii. He'd never attempted to follow through with any of his ideas*

because he always felt like he should focus on providing for his family. Although his children were now grown, and he and his wife were doing okay financially, he figured he should just keep working at his teaching job until he reached retirement age.

As Dale trudged on as a shop teacher, he struggled with his mood. He felt defeated and became depressed, something that he hadn't experienced before. He sought counseling, because he felt like there must be something wrong since for the first time in his career, he really wasn't enjoying his job.

Although Dale told me he agreed with his wife that he shouldn't venture into becoming an entrepreneur, it was clear that deep down he was still excited by the prospect. At the mere mention of opening his own furniture business, his face lit up, his body language changed, and his entire mood shifted.

We discussed his past experiences with taking risks. He said that years ago, he had invested in real estate and lost a lot of money. Ever since then he was scared to take any type of financial risk. After a few therapy sessions, Dale confessed that he'd still love to start a business, but he was terrified at the thought of giving up a stable job. He was confident in his woodworking skills but lacked business knowledge. We began discussing steps he could take to educate himself about the business world. Dale said he'd welcome the opportunity to take business classes at the local community college. He also said he'd be happy to join a local business networking group and would even look for a mentor to help him get started. With a few ideas in mind about how he still may be able to keep his dream alive, Dale continued weighing the pros and cons of opening his own business.

Within a few weeks, Dale made a decision—he would open his business on a part-time basis. He planned to start making furniture on nights and weekends in his garage. He already had much of what he would need to get the business started, but he would need to invest a little money for new materials. Overall, he felt confident he could start the business with relatively little investment cost. Initially he wouldn't have a storefront—he'd sell his furniture online and through the newspaper. If there was a lot of interest in his furniture, he'd consider opening a storefront at a later date, and perhaps he'd even be able to quit his job as a teacher altogether.

Dale's mood showed marked improvement as soon as he began thinking about turning his dream into a reality. After a few more therapy sessions, Dale appeared to continue doing better as he worked toward his goals. We scheduled one further appointment a month down the road just to make sure his mood remained stable. When he returned, he told me something quite interesting—not only had he started to make furniture for his business, but he was actually enjoying teaching shop class more than he ever had before. He said that the prospect of opening his own business seemed to spark his passion for teaching shop again. He planned to continue building furniture part-time but was no longer convinced he wanted to quit teaching. Instead, he was excited to teach his students the new things he was learning from his furniture business.

RISK AVERSION

We face many risks in our lives—financial, physical, emotional, social, and business risks to name a few, but often people avoid taking the risks that could help them reach their full potential because they're afraid. Do you respond positively to any of the points below?

☐ You struggle to make important decisions in your life.

☐ You spend a lot of time daydreaming about what you'd like to do, but you don't take any action.

☐ Sometimes you impulsively make a decision because thinking about the decision is just too anxiety provoking.

❏ You often think you could be doing a lot more adventurous and exciting things in life, but your fear holds you back.

❏ When you think about taking a risk, you usually only imagine the worst-case scenario and choose not to take the chance.

❏ You sometimes allow other people to make decisions for you so you don't have to make them.

❏ You avoid risks in at least some areas of your life—social, financial, or physical—because you're afraid.

❏ You base decisions on your level of fear. If you're a little afraid, you might do something. But, if you feel really afraid, you decide taking the risk is unwise.

❏ You think that outcomes are largely dependent on luck.

A lack of knowledge about how to calculate risk leads to increased fear. And fearing risk often leads to avoidance. But there are steps you can take to increase your ability to calculate risk accurately, and with practice, your risk-taking skills can improve.

WHY WE AVOID RISKS

When Dale pictured himself opening a business, he was reminded of the last time he took a financial risk and it didn't work out for him. His thoughts about taking another risk were immensely negative. He imagined himself becoming bankrupt or risking his entire retirement to open a business that would fail. His exaggeratedly negative thoughts led to fear and anxiety that prevented him from taking action. It never occurred to him to find ways to decrease his risk and increase his chances of success.

EMOTION PREVAILS OVER LOGIC

Even when our emotions lack any type of rational basis, we sometimes allow those feelings to prevail. Instead of thinking about "what could be . . ." we focus on "what if." But risks don't have to be reckless.

My yellow Lab, Jet, is a pretty emotional guy. The way he feels completely dictates his behavior. And for some reason, he is terrified of some pretty strange things. For example, he's scared of most types of flooring. He loves to walk around on carpet, but try to convince him to walk across linoleum, and you'll likely be out of luck. He's convinced himself that most floors are slippery and he's terrified he might fall.

Similar to how people often manage their anxiety, Jet created rules to manage his fears. He can walk across the hardwood flooring in my living room without a problem. But he won't set foot on the tile in the hallway. He used to stand at the end of the hallway and whine for hours because he wanted to visit me in the office but didn't want to risk stepping on the tile. I had hoped he'd ultimately decide visiting me was worth the risk, but he didn't. Eventually, I created a path of throw rugs and now he carefully steps from rug to rug to avoid walking on the floor.

He has rules about other houses that he occasionally visits. When he goes to Lincoln's mother's house, which also has tile, he proceeds to the living room by walking backward. In his canine mind, apparently it makes sense to back up, just not walk forward on her tile.

My dad took care of Jet once while we were out of town and he sat on the welcome mat just inside the door for the entire weekend. Sometimes Jet won't even enter certain buildings and has to be carried because he won't set foot on the linoleum. It's not a small feat to carry an eighty-pound dog into the vet's office, so sometimes we bring our own throw rugs to create a path for him.

Jet's fear usually outweighs his desire to risk walking on certain floors, but there is an exception to the rule—when there's cat food at stake, he's willing to take the risk. Jet had never actually entered the kitchen before because of the tile floor. But as soon as he figured out there was an unattended cat food dish, his excitement outweighed his fear.

Almost every day when he thinks we're not watching, Jet slowly puts one paw into the kitchen. Soon, he'll put two paws on the floor and stretch as far into the kitchen as he can. Eventually, he'll get three paws on the floor. With one last paw still on the carpet, he'll stretch as far as he can reach into the kitchen, and sometimes he manages to make it all the way to the cat food dish with all four paws safely on the tile.

I don't know how Jet draws conclusions about which floors are "safe" and which are "scary" simply by looking at them. Despite the lack of logic involved, it apparently makes sense to Jet.

Although it sounds ridiculous, humans often calculate risk in much the same way. We base our decisions on emotion instead of logic. We incorrectly assume there's a direct correlation between our fear level and the risk level. But often, our emotions are just not rational. If we truly understood how to calculate risk, we'd know which risks were worth taking and we'd be a lot less fearful about taking them.

WE DON'T THINK ABOUT RISKS

To calculate risk, we must predict the probability that the outcome of our behavior will result in either positive or negative consequences and then measure how big of an impact those consequences will have. Too often a risk evokes such a fear that we decide not to think about it or its consequences at all. And without understanding the potential outcomes of taking a risk, we usually end up avoiding risky ideas or dreams altogether.

Risk starts out as a thought process. Whether you're considering purchasing a new home, or you're deciding whether to put on your seat belt, the decision involves some level of risk. Your thoughts about the risk will influence the way you feel, and ultimately, sway your behavior. When you're driving your car, you decide how fast to go. You face safety and legal risks while driving on the road, and you must balance these risks with your time. The faster you drive, the less time you have to spend in the car, but driving faster will also increase your risk of getting in an accident and receiving legal consequences.

It's unlikely you spend much time thinking about how fast to drive on your way to work each day. Instead your decision to obey the law or break the speed limit weighs heavily on your usual routine. But if you're running late one day, you'll need to decide whether to drive faster and risk more physical and legal danger or risk being late for work.

The truth is, most of us don't really invest much time calculating which risks to take and which risks to avoid. Instead, we base our decisions on emotions or habit. If it sounds too scary, we avoid the risk. If we're excited about the possible benefits, we're more likely to overlook the risk.

THE PROBLEM WITH FEARING RISK

Once Dale's children had all graduated from college, he wanted to do more exciting things with his life. When he thought about opening a business, however, he felt like he'd be jumping off a cliff without a safety harness. What Dale didn't calculate was the emotional toll that avoiding risk was having on him. Not following his dream affected his mood because it changed the way he thought about himself and the way he felt about his teaching job.

YOU DON'T GET TO BE EXTRAORDINARY WITHOUT TAKING CALCULATED RISKS

Othmar Ammann was a Swiss-born engineer who immigrated to the United States. He started out as the chief engineer to the Port Authority of New York and within seven years, they promoted him to director of engineering. By all accounts, he had an important job.

But for as long as he could remember, Ammann had dreamed of becoming an architect. So he left his coveted job and set out to open his own business. In the years that followed, Ammann contributed to some of the most impressive American bridges, including the Verrazano-Narrows, the Delaware Memorial, and the Walt Whitman. His ability to design and create ornate, complicated, and extravagant structures earned him multiple awards.

Most impressive of all might be that Ammann was sixty years old when he switched careers. He continued to create architectural masterpieces right up until he was eighty-six. At an age when most people don't want to take any more risks, Ammann chose to take a calculated risk that allowed him to live his dream. If we only take risks that make us the most comfortable, we're likely missing out on some great opportunities. Taking calculated risks often mean the difference between living a mediocre life and living an extraordinary life.

EMOTION INTERFERES WITH MAKING LOGICAL CHOICES

You should have some fear about stepping into traffic. That fear reminds you that you should look both ways before you cross the road, so you can reduce the risk that you'll get hit by a car. If you didn't have any fear, you'd likely behave recklessly.

But our "fear meters" aren't always reliable. They sometimes go off even when we're not in any actual danger. And when we feel afraid, we tend to behave accordingly, falsely believing "If it feels scary, it must be too risky."

For years, we've been warned against the dangers of anything from killer bees to mad cow disease. It seems like we're constantly hearing various statistics, research studies, and warnings about so many perils that it becomes difficult to decipher the extent of danger we actually face in our lives. Take the research about cancer, for example. Some studies estimate cancer accounts for nearly one of every four deaths and other reports warn that within a few years about half of us will have cancer. Although those types of statistics can be a cause for alarm, they can often be misleading. A closer look at the numbers reveals a young healthy person who maintains a healthy lifestyle has a relatively low risk of developing cancer compared to an older, overweight person who smokes. But sometimes it's hard to put our personal level of risk into perspective when we're constantly bombarded with such frightening statistics.

Manufacturers of cleaning solutions have worked hard to convince us we need powerful chemicals, hand sanitizers, and antibacterial soaps to protect ourselves from germs. Media stories warn us that our kitchen countertops have more germs than our toilet seats as we're given visual reminders of how fast bacteria grows in a petri dish. Germaphobic people heed these warnings by taking drastic precautions to combat the risk of coming into contact with germs. They sanitize their homes daily with caustic chemicals, scrub their hands repeatedly with antibacterial products, and replace handshakes with fist bumps to reduce the spread of germs. But attempts to win the war on germs may actually do more harm than good. In fact, there's research that shows getting rid of too many germs reduces our ability to build immunity from illness. A study from Johns Hopkins Children's Center found that newborns who were exposed to germs, pet and rodent dander, and roach allergens were less likely to develop asthma and allergies. Fear leads many people to incorrectly assume that germs pose a much higher risk than they actually do, because in the reality, bacteria-free environments may pose a greater threat to our health than the germs.

It's important to be aware of your emotions throughout the decision-making process. If you're feeling sad, you're likely to anticipate failure and avoid the risk. If you're feeling happy, you may disregard the risk and forge ahead. There's even research that shows that fear of something completely unrelated to the risk can influence your decision. If you're stressed about your job, and you're also considering purchasing a new home, you'll be more likely to view that home purchase as a bigger risk than if you weren't feeling stressed at work. Often, we're not good at separating what factors are influencing our feelings so we lump them all together.

CALCULATE RISKS AND REDUCE FEAR

It had never before occurred to Dale that he didn't have to dive into a business headfirst. Once he began identifying ways to reduce the chances that he'd go bankrupt, he felt relieved and was able to think more logically about how he could turn his business into a reality. Clearly, there was a chance that he may not ever earn back the money he invested in starting the business, but after thinking it through, that was a calculated risk he was willing to accept.

BALANCE EMOTION WITH LOGIC

Don't get fooled into thinking that your anxiety level should be the factor that helps you make the final decision about risk.

Your feelings may be very unreliable. The more emotional you feel, the less logical your thoughts will be. Increase your rational thoughts about the risk you're facing to balance out your emotional reaction.

Many people are terrified to fly in airplanes. Often, this fear stems from a lack of control. The pilot is in control, not the passengers, and this lack of control instills fear. Many potential passengers are so afraid they choose to drive great distances to get to a destination instead of flying. But their decision to drive is based solely on emotion, not logic. Logic says that statistically, the odds of dying in a car crash are around 1 in 5,000, while the odds of dying in a plane crash are closer to 1 in 11 million.

If you're going to take a risk, especially one that could possibly involve your well-being, wouldn't you want the odds in your favor? However, most people choose the option that will cause them the least amount of anxiety. Pay attention to the thoughts you have about taking the risk and make sure you're basing your decision on facts, not just feelings.

Most of the research shows that we are pretty bad at accurately calculating risk. Frighteningly, many of our major life decisions are based on complete irrationality:

- *We incorrectly judge how much control we have over a situation.* We're usually more willing to take bigger risks when we think we have more control. Most people feel more comfortable when they're in the driver's seat of a car for example, but just because you're in the driver's seat doesn't mean you can avoid an accident.

- *We overcompensate when safeguards are in place.* We behave more recklessly when we think there are safety nets in place, and ultimately, we increase our risk. People tend to speed more when they wear their seat belts. And insurance companies discovered that increased safety features on cars actually correlated with higher accident rates.

- *We don't recognize the difference between skill and chance.* Casinos have discovered that when gamblers play craps, they roll the dice differently depending on what type of number they need to win. When they want to roll a high number, they throw the dice hard. When they want a small number, they roll the dice softly. Even though it's a game of chance, people behave as if it involves some level of skill.

- *We are influenced by our superstitious beliefs.* Whether a business leader wears his lucky socks or a person reads his horoscope before leaving the house, superstitions impact our willingness to take risks. On average, ten thousand fewer people fly on Friday the thirteenth, and black cats are less likely to get adopted from a shelter on that day. Although research shows most people think crossing their fingers increases their luck, in reality, it does nothing to mitigate risk.

- *We become easily deluded when we see a potentially large payoff.* Even when the odds are stacked against you, if you really like the potential payoff, like in the lottery for example, you'll likely overestimate your odds of success.

- *We grow comfortable with familiarity.* The more often we take a risk, the more we tend to miscalculate how big of a risk we're actually taking. If you take the same risk over and over again, you'll stop perceiving it as risky. If you speed on your way to work every day, you'll greatly underestimate the danger you're putting yourself in.

- *We place a lot of faith in other people's abilities to perceive risk.* Emotions can be contagious. If you're in a crowd of people who don't react to the smell of smoke, it's likely you might not sense much danger. In contrast, if other people begin to panic, you're much more likely to react.

- *We can be influenced by the media in how we perceive risk.* If you are constantly exposed to news stories about a rare disease, you're more likely to think your chances of contracting the disease are higher, even if all the news stories are only reporting on isolated incidents. Similarly, stories about natural disasters or tragic events can cause you to feel you are at a greater risk of catastrophe than you actually are.

MINIMIZE RISK MAXIMIZE SUCCESS

Every year at my high school's graduation ceremony the valedictorian was expected to give a speech. Halfway through my senior year, when I learned I was going to be the valedictorian, my fear of giving a speech outweighed my excitement about having the highest GPA in my class. I was incredibly shy, to the point that I usually didn't speak in class, even though my classmates were people I'd known since kindergarten. The thought of standing at a podium and giving a speech in front of a packed auditorium was enough to make me weak in the knees.

When I tried writing my speech, I had no words to put down on the paper. I was too distracted by the thought of having to speak the words in front of a crowd of people. But I knew I had to get something together, because the clock was ticking.

And common advice like "Picture the audience in their underwear" or "Practice reading your speech in front of a mirror" wasn't going to be enough to calm my nerves. I was terrified.

So I spent some time thinking about what my biggest fear with public speaking actually was. And it turns out, I was afraid of the audience's rejection. I kept imagining that after I had finished my speech, the audience would remain completely silent, because whatever I had just mumbled was either completely inaudible or so horribly presented that no one could muster a clap. So, to mitigate my risk, I had a conversation with my best friends and they helped me devise a brilliant plan.

The plan reduced my risk and nerves enough that I was able to write my speech. A few weeks later, on graduation day, I was feeling incredibly nervous as I stood at the podium. My voice cracked the entire time, as I offered whatever advice an eighteen-year-old could possibly offer her fellow classmates. But I got through it. And when I was done, my friends followed through with our plan. On cue, they stood up and cheered like they'd just witnessed the best rock concert in the world. And what happens when a few people in a room stand up to applaud? Other people follow suit. I received a standing ovation.

Was it earned? Maybe. Probably not. And to this day, that part doesn't really matter to me. The point was, I knew if I could get rid of my biggest fear—that no one would clap for me—I could get through the speech.

The level of risk you'll experience in a given situation is unique to you. While speaking in front of a group is a risk to some people, it's not risky at all to others. Ask yourself the following questions to help you calculate your risk level:

- *What are the potential costs?* Sometimes the cost of taking a risk is tangible—like the money you might spend on an investment—but other times, intangible costs are associated with risk, like the risk of being rejected.

- *What are the potential benefits?* Consider the potential positive outcome of taking the risk. Look at what would happen if the risk turns out well. Do you stand to gain increased finances? Better relationships? Improved health? There needs to be a big enough payoff to outweigh the potential costs.

- *How will this help me achieve my goal?* It is important to examine your bigger goals and look at how this risk plays into that goal. For example, if you are hoping to gain more money, look at how opening your own business could help you with that goal as you examine your risk.

- *What are the alternatives?* Sometimes we look at risk as if we only have two choices—take the risk or pass it up. But, often, there are many different types of opportunities that can help you reach your goals. It's important to recognize those alternatives that may lie in between so you can make the most well-informed decision.

- *How good would it be if the best-case scenario came true?* Spend some time really thinking about the payoff in a risk and how that payoff could impact your life. Try to develop realistic expectations for how the best-case scenario could benefit you.

- *What is the worst thing that could happen and how could I reduce the risk it will occur?* It's also important to really examine the worst-possible scenario and then think about steps you could take to minimize the risk that it would happen. For example, if you are considering investing in a business, how could you increase your chance for success?

- *How bad would it be if the worst-case scenario did come true?* Just like hospitals, cities, and governments have disaster-preparedness plans, it can be helpful to create your own. Develop a plan for how you could respond if the worst-case scenario did occur.

- *How much will this decision matter in five years?* To help you keep things in perspective, ask yourself how much this particular risk is likely to impact your future. If it's a small risk, you probably won't even remember it a few years from now. If it's a big risk, it could greatly impact your future.

It can be helpful to write down your answers so you can review them and read them over. Be willing to do more research and gain as much information as possible when you don't have the facts available to help you calculate a risk properly. When the information is not available, resolve to make the best decision you can with the information you have.

PRACTICE TAKING RISKS

Prior to his death in 2007, *Psychology Today* named Albert Ellis the "greatest living psychologist." Ellis was known for teaching people how to challenge their self-defeating thoughts and beliefs. He didn't just teach these principles, he also lived them.

As a young man, Ellis was incredibly shy and he feared talking to women. He was terrified of getting rejected, so he avoided ever asking a woman out on a date. But, ultimately, he knew that rejection wasn't the worst thing in the world and decided to face his fears.

He went to a local botanical garden every day for a month. Whenever he saw a woman sitting by herself on a bench, he sat next to her. He forced himself to start up a conversation within one minute of sitting down. In that month, he found 130 opportunities to speak with women and of those 130, 30 women got up and walked away as soon as he sat down. But he started conversations with the rest. Out of the 100 women he invited on a date, one said yes—however, she didn't show up. But Ellis didn't despair. Instead, it reinforced to him that he could tolerate taking risks even when he feared rejection.

By facing his fears, Ellis recognized his irrational thoughts that had made him more fearful of taking risks. Understanding how these thoughts influenced his feelings helped him later develop new therapy techniques that would help other people challenge their irrational thinking.

Like Ellis, monitor the outcome of the risks that you take. Take notice of how you felt before, during, and after taking a risk. Ask yourself what you learned and how you can apply that knowledge to future decisions.

TAKING CALCULATED RISKS MAKES YOU STRONGER

Richard Branson, founder of the United Kingdom–based Virgin Group, is known for taking risks. After all, you don't get to own four hundred companies without taking some leaps along the way. But he's taken calculated risks that have certainly paid off for him.

As a child, Branson struggled in school. He had dyslexia and his academic performance suffered. But he didn't let that hold him back. Instead, as a young teen he started business ventures. At the age of fifteen, he began a bird-breeding business.

His business pursuits quickly grew as he went on to own record companies, airlines, and mobile phone companies. His empire has expanded to a current net worth estimated to be around $5 billion. Although he could easily sit back and enjoy the fruits of his labor, Branson loves to continue challenging himself and his employees every day.

"At Virgin, I use two techniques to free our team from the same old routine: breaking records and making bets," Branson wrote in an article for *Entrepreneur* magazine. "Taking chances is a great way to test myself and our group, and also push boundaries while having fun together." And push boundaries he does. His teams create products that people say won't work. They break records that people claim are impossible. And they accept challenges that no one else attempts. But through it all, Branson acknowledges his risks are "strategic judgments, not blind gambles."

Success won't find you. You have to pursue it. Stepping into the unknown to take carefully calculated risks can help you reach your dreams and fulfill your goals.

TROUBLESHOOTING AND COMMON TRAPS

Monitor the type of risks you're taking and how you feel about those risks. Also, take note about which opportunities you are passing up. This can help ensure that you are taking the risks that could benefit you the most, even the kind that cause some anxiety. Remember that calculating risks takes practice, but with practice, you can learn and grow.

WHAT'S HELPFUL

Being aware of emotional reactions to risk taking

Identifying types of risks that are particularly challenging

Recognizing irrational thoughts that influence your decision making

Educating yourself about the facts

Spending time calculating each risk before making a decision

Practicing taking risks and monitoring the results so you can learn from each risk you take

WHAT'S NOT HELPFUL

Basing your decisions about risk on how you feel

Avoiding the types of risk that stir up the most fear

Allowing irrational thoughts to influence your willingness to try something new

Ignoring the facts or not making an effort to learn more when you lack the information you need to make the best choice

Reacting impulsively without taking time to weigh the risk

Refusing to take risks that cause you discomfort

CHAPTER 7

THEY DON'T DWELL ON THE PAST

We do not heal the past by dwelling there; we heal the past by living fully in the present.
—MARIANNE WILLIAMSON

Gloria was a hardworking fifty-five-year-old woman who had been referred to counseling after telling her doctor that she was feeling extremely stressed. Her twenty-eight-year-old daughter had recently moved back in with her again. Since moving out of Gloria's home at eighteen she'd been back at least a dozen times. She'd usually find a new boyfriend and within weeks, if not days, of meeting him, she'd move in with him. But it never worked out and she'd always move back in with Gloria.

Gloria's daughter was unemployed and she wasn't actively looking for work. She spent her days watching TV and surfing the Internet. She couldn't be bothered to help out around the house, or even clean up after herself. Although Gloria said she felt like she was offering hotel and maid services, she always welcomed her daughter to stay with her.

She thought giving her daughter a place to stay was the least she could do. She hadn't given her daughter the childhood she most likely deserved, and she admitted she hadn't been a very good mother. After she and her husband divorced, Gloria had dated a lot of men, and many of them weren't healthy role models. Gloria now understood she'd invested too much energy into drinking and dating rather than parenting. And she felt like the mistakes she made were the reason her daughter was struggling so much now. It was clear from the start that Gloria's shame over the way she'd parented led her to enable her daughter now that she was an adult. The majority of Gloria's stress stemmed from her anxiety over her daughter's immature behavior. She worried about her daughter's future and she wanted her to be able to have a job and live independently.

The more we talked, the more Gloria recognized that her shame and guilt were interfering with her ability to be a good parent now. She had to forgive herself and stop dwelling on the past if she wanted to move forward and do what was best for her daughter. When I asked her to consider the likelihood that her daughter would simply wake up one day and start behaving responsibly given the current conditions, Gloria acknowledged that wasn't going to happen but she wasn't sure what to do.

Over the next few weeks, we explored how Gloria viewed the past. Whenever she thought about her daughter's childhood, she'd think things like I am such a bad person for not always putting my daughter's needs first or It's my fault my daughter has so many problems. We explored her thoughts, and slowly but surely, Gloria learned how her self-condemnation influenced the way she treated her daughter in the present.

Gradually, Gloria began to accept the reality that while she wasn't an idyllic mother, punishing herself for that today would not change the past. She also began to recognize that her current behavior toward her daughter wasn't making amends but instead enabling her daughter's self-destructive behavior.

Armed with her new attitude, Gloria created some rules and set limits with her daughter. She told her that she could only remain living in her home if she were actively looking for work. She was willing to give her some time to get back on her feet, but starting in two months, she'd need to pay rent if she were going to continue living at home. Although her daughter *was initially upset with Gloria's new rules, she began looking for work within a few days.*

Within a few weeks Gloria entered my office to proudly announce that her daughter had a job and unlike some of the other jobs she'd had before, this one could become a career. She said she'd seen huge changes in her daughter since she was offered this job and she was talking a lot more about her future aspirations. Although Gloria hadn't yet completely forgiven herself for the past, she recognized that the only thing worse than being a bad parent for eighteen years would be to be a bad parent for another eighteen years.

STUCK IN HISTORY

Sometimes people dwell on the things that happened years ago, while others tend to dwell on whatever happened last week. Do any of these scenarios sound familiar?

❒ You wish you could press the rewind button so you could redo portions of your life.

❒ You struggle with major regrets about your past.

❒ You spend a lot of time wondering how life would have turned out if only you had chosen a slightly different path.

❒ You sometimes feel like the best days of your life are already behind you.

❒ You replay past memories in your mind like a scene from a movie over and over again.

❒ You sometimes imagine saying or doing something differently in past memories to try and create a different outcome.

❏ You punish yourself or convince yourself you don't deserve to be happy.

❏ You feel ashamed of your past.

❏ When you make a mistake or experience an embarrassing episode, you keep repeatedly replaying the event in your mind.

❏ You invest a lot of time in thinking about all the things you "should have" or "could have" done differently.

Although self-reflection is healthy, dwelling can be self-destructive, preventing you from enjoying the present and planning for the future. But you don't have to stay stuck in the past. You can choose to start living in the moment.

WHY WE DWELL ON THE PAST

Gloria's daughter often manipulated her mother by preying on her guilt, reminding Gloria that she wasn't always there for her as a child, which only fueled Gloria's remorse. If her daughter hadn't yet forgiven her, how could Gloria possibly forgive herself? She accepted her feelings of constant guilt as part of her penance for the mistakes she'd made, and as a result she continued to dwell on the past.

Lingering guilt, shame, and anger are just a few of the feelings that can keep you stuck in the past. You might subconsciously think, *If I stay miserable long enough, I'll eventually be able to forgive myself.* You may not even be aware that deep down, you don't believe you deserve happiness.

THE FEAR OF MOVING FORWARD MAKES US WANT TO STAY STUCK IN THE PAST

Two weeks after my mother passed away, my dad's house caught on fire. The fire was contained to the basement, but smoke and black soot permeated throughout the house. Everything in the entire house had to be cleaned from top to bottom by a crew hired by the insurance company. All my mother's belongings were handled by complete strangers. And it bothered me.

I had wanted things to stay just the way my mother had left them. I wanted her clothes to stay hung in the closet the same way she had arranged them. I wanted her Christmas decorations to stay in the boxes in the same way she'd organized them. I wanted to someday—way down the road—open her jewelry box and see how she had last placed her jewelry. But we didn't have that luxury. Instead, everything got rearranged. Her clothes no longer smelled like her. I had no way of even knowing what the last book was that she was reading. And we'd never be able to sort through her belongings at our own pace.

A few years later when Lincoln died, I again wanted everything to stay frozen in time. I felt like if I studied the way he kept his clothing hung in the closet, or if I could figure out which order he'd read his books in, I'd be able to learn more about him, even though he was gone. I thought that if things got moved around, thrown out, or reorganized, I'd lose my opportunity to study valuable clues that could give me more insight and information about him.

It was as if I could keep him with me if I made sure there were always more things to learn. Maybe a scrap of paper would have a note on it. Or maybe I'd find a picture I'd never seen before. I wanted to somehow create new memories that included Lincoln, even though he wasn't there. Although we'd been together for six years, it just wasn't enough. I wasn't ready to let go of anything that reminded me of him. I thought I'd be leaving him behind if I got rid of his belongings that I no longer needed, and I didn't want that.

My attempts to keep everything frozen in time didn't work. Obviously, the rest of the world kept going. And over the course of many months, I was able to begin to let go of my desire to keep everything as if it were in a time capsule. Slowly, I would reassure myself that it was okay to throw away something with Lincoln's handwriting on it. And I started to get rid of the magazines he kept receiving in the mail. But I have to admit, it took me two years to finally throw away his toothbrush. I knew he didn't need it, but somehow throwing it away almost seemed like a betrayal. It seemed more comfortable to dwell in the past, because that's where Lincoln, and my memories of him, lived. But to stay stuck there, while the rest of the world changed and moved forward, wasn't healthy or helpful. I had to trust that moving forward wouldn't cause me to forget any of my wonderful memories.

Even though as a therapist I help people work on their rational thinking, grief brought on a lot of irrational thoughts. It made me want to dwell on the past, because the past was where Lincoln was alive. But if I had spent all my time thinking about the past, I'd have never been able to create new and happy memories again.

DWELLING ON THE PAST DISTRACTS YOU FROM THE PRESENT

It's not just sad or tragic events that leave people focused on the past. Sometimes we dwell on the past as a way to distract ourselves from the present. Perhaps you know that forty-year-old former high school quarterback who still squeezes into his varsity jacket and talks about his "old glory days." Or maybe you're friends with the thirty-five-year-old mom who still lists "prom queen" as one of her biggest accomplishments. Often, we romanticize the past as a way to escape problems in the present.

If, for example, you're not happy in your current relationship, or if you're not in a relationship at all, it may be tempting to spend a lot of time thinking about a past love. Perhaps you wish that your last relationship had worked out or you still think if you'd married your high school sweetheart, you'd be better off.

It can be tempting to fixate on how much easier or happier life was "back then." You may even begin to regret some of the decisions you made that landed you where you are today and say things like "If only I'd married my old boyfriend, I'd still be happy"; "If I hadn't dropped out of college, I'd have a job I love"; or "If I didn't agree to move to a new city, I'd still have a good life." The truth is, we don't know what life would have had in store for us had we not made those choices. But it's easy for us to imagine that life could be better if we could only change the past.

THE PROBLEM WITH DWELLING ON THE PAST

Gloria couldn't see her daughter as a capable adult; all she could see were her own mistakes. Her guilt prevented her from focusing on the present and as a result, she enabled her daughter's irresponsible behavior. Unfortunately, her daughter was repeating a lot of the same mistakes Gloria had made. Dwelling on the past was not only holding Gloria back from reaching her full potential, but it was also holding her daughter back from maturing into a responsible adult.

Ruminating on the past won't change it. Instead, wasting your time dwelling on what's already happened will only lead to more problems in the future. Here are some of the ways that dwelling on the past can interfere with your ability to be your best self:

- *You miss out on the present.* You can't enjoy the present if your mind is constantly stuck in the past. You'll miss out on experiencing new opportunities and celebrating the joys of today if you're distracted by things that have already occurred.

- *Dwelling on the past makes it impossible to adequately prepare for the future.* You won't be able to clearly define your goals or stay motivated to create change when a big part of you remains stuck in the past.

- *Dwelling on the past interferes with your decision-making skills.* When you have unresolved issues from the past, those conflicts will cloud your thinking. You won't be able to adequately make healthy decisions about what's best for you today when you can't get over something that happened yesterday.

- *Dwelling on the past doesn't solve anything.* Replaying the same scripts in your head and focusing on things you no longer have control over won't resolve anything.

- *Dwelling on the past can lead to depression.* Ruminating on negative events conjures up negative emotions. And when you feel sad, the more likely you are to conjure up even more sad memories. Dwelling on past times can be a vicious cycle that keeps you stuck in the same emotional state.

- *Romanticizing the past—the grass-is-greener philosophy—isn't helpful.* It's easy to convince yourself that you felt happier, more confident, and completely carefree back then. But there's a good chance you're exaggerating how great things used to be. It can also make you exaggerate how bad things are now.

- *Dwelling on the past is bad for your physical health.* Thinking constantly about negative events increases inflammation in your body, according to a 2013 study conducted by researchers at the University of Ohio. Dwelling on the past could put you at a greater risk for diseases associated with heart disease, cancer, and dementia.

STOP THE PAST FROM HOLDING YOU BACK

Once Gloria recognized that she could learn from her past, rather than just beating herself up over it, her thinking shifted. She began changing her behavior and the way she parented her daughter. This helped her recognize how her past mistakes taught her valuable lessons about parenting. Over the course of a couple of months she was able to recall her earlier parenting mistakes without an overwhelming sense of shame.

SHIFT YOUR THINKING

Dwelling starts out as a cognitive process, but eventually it influences your emotions and behavior. By shifting the way you think about the past, you can move forward.

- *Schedule time to think about a past event.* Sometimes our brains need a chance to sort things out and the more you tell yourself not to think about it, the more those memories can crop up throughout the day. Instead of battling to suppress the memories, remind yourself, *I can think about that after dinner tonight.* Then, after dinner, give yourself twenty minutes to think about it. When your time is up, move on to something else.

- *Give yourself something else to think about.* Create a plan to help you think about something else. For example, decide that whenever you think about that job you didn't get, you'll shift your focus to thinking about planning your next vacation. This can be especially helpful if you're prone to dwell on the negative right before you go to sleep at night.

- *Establish goals for the future.* It's impossible to dwell on the past if you're planning for the future. Establish both short-term and long-term goals and begin working on the action steps needed to achieve those goals. It will give you something to look forward to while also preventing you from looking too much into the past.

Our memories aren't as accurate as we think they are. Often, when we recall unpleasant events, we exaggerate and catastrophize them. If you think about something you said during a meeting that you later regretted, you may envision that other people were reacting much more negatively than they actually did. When you recall negative memories, try these strategies to keep your experiences in perspective:

- *Focus on the lessons you learned.* If you've endured hard times, focus on what you've learned from that experience. Accept that it happened and think about how you may be a changed person because of it, but realize that doesn't necessarily have to be a bad thing. Maybe you learned to speak up because you allowed yourself to be treated poorly, or perhaps you learned that you need to be honest if you want relationships to last. Some of the best life lessons can be learned from the toughest times you've endured.

- *Think about the facts, not the emotion.* Thinking about negative events can be very distressing because you'll likely focus on how you felt during the event. But if you recall an event by walking yourself through the facts and details of the memory, your distress decreases. Instead of dwelling on how you felt when you went to a funeral, recall specific details about where you sat, what you wore, who was there. When you begin to take away the emotion surrounding an event, you're less likely to dwell on it.

- *Look at the situation differently.* When you review your past, examine what other ways there are to look at the same situation. You have control over how you weave the story. The same story can be told countless ways and still be true. If your current version is upsetting, see how else you can look at it. For example, Gloria could have reminded herself that her daughter's current choices weren't all related to her childhood. She could have recognized that although she may have made some mistakes, she was not responsible for the choices her daughter was making now.

MAKE PEACE WITH THE PAST

When James Barrie was six years old, his thirteen-year-old brother, David, died in an ice skating accident. Although his mother had ten children total, it was no secret that David had been her favorite. After his death, she was so distraught she could hardly cope with life.

So at the age of six, Barrie did everything he could to compensate for his mother's grief. He even tried to take over the role of David to help fill the void his mother felt from his death. He dressed in David's clothing and learned how to whistle the same way David used to. He became her constant companion as he devoted his entire childhood to trying to make his mother smile again.

Despite Barrie's attempts to make his mother happy, she often warned him about the hardships of being an adult. She told him to never grow up because adulthood was only filled with grief and unhappiness. She even said she took some relief knowing that David would never have to grow up and face the realities of adulthood.

In an attempt to please his mother, Barrie resisted maturity as much as he could. He especially didn't want to grow any older than David had been when he'd passed away. He tried with all his might to remain a child. His attempts to stay a boy even seemed to stunt his physical growth as he hardly reached five feet tall.

After he finished school, Barrie wanted to become an author. But his family pressured him to go on to study at a university, because that's what David would have done. So Barrie found a compromise—he'd continue his education but he'd study literature.

Barrie went on to pen one of the most famous works of children's literature, *Peter Pan, or the Boy Who Wouldn't Grow Up.* Originally written as a play, which later became a famous movie, the main character, Peter Pan, faces the conflict between the innocence of childhood and the responsibility of adulthood. Peter chooses to remain a child and encourages all the other children to do the same. As the legendary fairy tale, it seems like a delightful

children's story. But when you know the author's history, the an-
ecdote is quite tragic.

Barrie's mother couldn't move forward after the death of her
son. She was convinced that childhood was the best time of her
life and that the present and future were only riddled with pain
and agony. As an extreme case of someone who dwelled on the
past, she allowed it to interfere with the well-being of her children. It affected Barrie not just during his childhood, but also
throughout his adulthood.

The misconceptions we hold about grief can contribute to our
choice to live in the past. Many people wrongly believe that the
amount of time you grieve over someone is directly proportional
to the amount of love you had for someone. If you cared a little
about someone who died, you may grieve for months. But if you
really loved that person, you'd grieve for years or even for the rest
of your life. But the truth is, there isn't a right amount of time to
grieve. In fact, you may grieve for years, or even forever, but the
amount of sadness you feel doesn't equate to the amount of love
you had for that person.

Hopefully, you have many cherished memories of your loved
one. But moving forward means actively working toward creating
new memories for yourself, making the best decisions for you, and
not always doing what someone else would want you to do.

If you find yourself ruminating on some aspect of your past,
you may need to take action to make peace with the past. Here are
some ways to make peace with the past:

- *Give yourself permission to move forward.* Sometimes you
  just need to give yourself permission to move forward.
  Moving forward doesn't mean you have to leave your
  memories of a loved one behind, but it does mean you
  can do the things you need to do to enjoy the moment
  and get the most you can out of life.

- *Recognize the emotional toll of dwelling on the past versus moving forward.* Sometimes dwelling on the past is a strategy that works in the short term but not in the long term. If you think about the past, you don't have to focus on what's going on right now. But, over the long term, there are consequences. Recognize what you'll miss out on in life if your attention is focused on the past.

- *Practice forgiveness.* Whether you're dwelling on past hurt and anger because you can't forgive yourself or because you can't forgive someone else, forgiveness can help you let go of that hurt. Forgiveness doesn't mean forgetting something happened. If someone hurt you, you can forgive them while still deciding not to have any more contact, for example. Instead, focus on letting go so you don't stay consumed with the hurt and anger.

- *Change behavior that keeps you stuck in the past.* If you find yourself avoiding certain activities—because you are afraid it will drudge up bad memories or because you feel like you don't deserve to do them—consider doing them anyway. You can't change the past. But you can choose to accept it. If you've made mistakes, you can't go back and fix them or erase them. You may be able to try and take steps to repair some of the damage you've caused, but it won't make everything better.

- *Seek professional help if necessary.* Sometimes traumatic events can lead to mental health issues, like post-traumatic stress disorder. Near-death experiences, for example, can lead to flashbacks and nightmares that make it difficult to make peace with the past. Professional counseling can help reduce the distress associated with traumatic memories so you can move forward more productively.

HOW MAKING PEACE WITH THE PAST WILL MAKE YOU STRONGER

Wynona Ward grew up in rural Vermont. Her family was poor, and as in many homes in the area, domestic violence was common. Ward's father routinely physically and sexually abused her. She often witnessed her father beating her mother. Although doctors treated her mother's wounds and neighbors heard their screams, no one ever intervened.

Ward kept her family problems a secret. She immersed herself in her academics and excelled in school. At the age of seventeen, she left home and got married. She and her husband became over-the-road truck drivers.

After sixteen years of traveling the country as a truck driver, Ward learned that her older brother had abused a young family member. It was at that moment that she decided that she had to do something. She decided to go back to school so she could help put an end to the generational abuse that was going on within her family.

Ward enrolled in the University of Vermont and studied from the truck while her husband drove. She completed her degree and went on to further her education at Vermont Law School. Upon getting her law degree, she used a small grant to start Have Justice Will Travel, an organization that serves families in rural areas affected by domestic violence.

Ward provides rural domestic violence victims with free legal representation. She also connects them with the appropriate social services. Because many families lack the resources or transportation to travel to an office, Ward travels to them. She provides education and services that help families put an end to generational cycles of abuse. Instead of dwelling on her horrific past, Ward chooses to focus on what she can do to help other people in the present.

Refusing to dwell on the past doesn't mean you pretend the past didn't happen. In fact, it often means embracing and accepting your experiences so you can live in the present. Doing so frees up your mental energy and allows you to plan for your future based on who you want to become, not who you used to be. Anger, shame, and guilt can run your life if you're not careful. Letting go of those emotions helps you to be in charge of your life.

TROUBLESHOOTING AND COMMON TRAPS

If you spend all your time looking in the rearview mirror, you can't look out the windshield. Staying stuck in the past will prevent you from enjoying the future. Recognize times when you're dwelling on the past and take the steps necessary to heal your emotions so you can move forward.

WHAT'S HELPFUL

Reflecting on the past enough that you can learn from it

Moving forward in your life, even when it may be painful to do so

Actively working through grief so you can focus on the present and plan for the future

Thinking about negative events in terms of facts, not emotions

Finding ways to make peace with the past

WHAT'S NOT HELPFUL

Trying to pretend the past didn't happen

Trying to prevent yourself from moving forward in life

Focusing on what you've lost in life without being able to live in the present

Replaying painful events in your mind repeatedly and focusing on how you felt during them

Trying to undo the past or make up for your past mistakes

CHAPTER 8

THEY DON'T MAKE THE SAME MISTAKES OVER AND OVER

*The only real mistake is the one
from which we learn nothing.*
—JOHN POWELL

When Kristy entered my therapy office, the first thing she said was, "I have a college degree and I'm smart enough not to yell at my co-workers. So why can't I stop yelling at my kids?" Every morning she made a promise that she wasn't going to yell at her two teenagers. But almost every evening she found herself raising her voice toward at least one of them.

She told me she yelled because she felt frustrated when her kids didn't listen to her. And lately, it seemed like they hardly ever listened. Her thirteen-year-old daughter often refused to do her chores and her fifteen-year-old son wasn't putting any effort into his homework. Whenever Kristy came home from a long day at work to find them watching TV and playing video games, she told them to get to work. But they usually talked back and Kristy resorted to yelling.

Kristy clearly knew that yelling wasn't good for her kids. She recognized that it only made the situation worse. She prided herself on being an

intelligent and successful person, so it surprised her when s.
get this area of her life under control.

Kristy spent a couple of sessions examining why she kept making
same mistake over and over. She discovered that she really didn't know how
to discipline the kids without yelling, and she wasn't going to be able to
stop yelling at her kids until she had a plan about what to do instead. So
we worked on various strategies she could use to respond to disrespectful and
defiant behavior. Kristy decided she'd offer one warning, and then follow
through with a consequence if her kids didn't do as she asked.

She also needed to learn how to recognize when she was getting angry,
so she could step away from a situation before she started yelling. Her
downfall seemed to be that when she lost her cool, her rational thoughts
about discipline went out the window.

I further worked with Kristy to help her find a new way to think about
discipline. When she first came to me, she admitted that she felt it was
her responsibility to make her kids do what she said, at all costs, because
if they didn't, it would mean they won. But this approach always seemed
to backfire. Once Kristy could let go of the idea she needed to win a power
struggle, she developed a new outlook on discipline. If her children chose not
to follow her directions, she took away their electronics without arguing and
trying to force them to behave.

It took some practice for Kristy to change her parenting strategies. There
were times where she still found herself resorting to yelling, but she was now
equipped with alternative discipline strategies. Each time she found herself
slipping, she could review her triggers and identify strategies to prevent
raising her voice again the next time.

REPEAT OFFENDER

Although we'd like to think we learn from our mistakes the first time
around, the truth is, everyone repeats mistakes sometimes. That's just
part of being human. Mistakes can be behavioral—like showing up

late for work—or they can be cognitive. Thinking errors include always assuming people don't like you or never planning ahead. Although someone may say "Next time I won't jump to conclusions," they may repeat those same thinking errors if they're not careful. Do any of the points below sound familiar?

☐ You often find yourself stuck at the same point when you're trying to reach a goal.

☐ When you encounter an obstacle, you don't invest much time looking for new ways to overcome it.

☐ You find it hard to give up your bad habits because you keep falling back on your old ways.

☐ You don't invest much time in analyzing why your attempts to reach your goals are unsuccessful.

☐ You get mad at yourself because you can't get rid of some of your bad habits.

☐ You sometimes say things like "I'll never do that again," only to find yourself doing the same thing all over again.

☐ Sometimes it just feels like it takes too much effort to learn new ways to do things.

☐ You often feel frustrated by your lack of self-discipline.

☐ Your motivation to do things differently disappears as soon as you begin to feel uncomfortable or upset.

Did any of those points resonate with you? Sometimes we just don't learn the first time. But there are steps we can take to avoid repeating the unhealthy mistakes that hold us back from reaching our goals.

WHY WE MAKE THE SAME MISTAKES

Despite her frustration, Kristy had never truly thought about why she yelled or what alternatives could be more effective. Initially, she was hesitant to follow through with a new discipline plan because she worried that removing privileges would only anger her children further and lead to more disrespectful behavior. She had to gain confidence in her parenting abilities before she could stop repeating the same mistakes.

If someone says "I'm never going to do that again," why on earth would the person keep doing it over and over? The truth is, our behavior is complicated.

For a long time, many teachers held the common belief that if a child was allowed to guess an answer incorrectly, she would be in danger of accidently memorizing the wrong answer. For example, if a child guessed that $4 + 4 = 6$, she'd always recall 6 as the right answer, even after she was corrected. To prevent this, teachers gave kids the answers first without allowing them to make an educated guess.

Fast-forward to 2012, when a research study published in the *Journal of Experimental Psychology: Learning, Memory, and Cognition* showed that as long as study participants were given a chance to learn the correct information, they could learn from previous mistakes. In fact, researchers found that when kids thought about potential answers, even if those answers were incorrect, their retention rates for the correct answers improved once their mistakes were corrected. Kids, just like adults, are able to learn from their mistakes when they're given the opportunity.

Despite the fact that we now have a study that proves we can learn from our mistakes, it is difficult to completely unlearn what we were taught when we were younger. Growing up, you may have learned it's better to hide your mistakes than face the consequences. And school wasn't the only place we built our under-standing of handling mistakes. Celebrities, politicians, and athletes are commonly portrayed in the media as trying to cover up their missteps. They lie and attempt to talk their way out of admit-ting they did anything wrong even when there's evidence to the contrary. And when we deny our mistakes, we are less likely to examine them and gain any true understanding or lessons from them, making us more susceptible to repeating them in the future. We've all heard this line before: "I stand by my decisions . . ." This is an acknowledgment of behavior but falls short of admitting a mistake, all because of pride.

Being stubborn is a big factor for repeat offenders too. A person who makes a poor investment may say "Well, I've got so much in-vested in this now; I might as well just keep going." Rather than just losing a little money, he'd rather risk more because he's too stubborn to stop. Someone in a job she despises may say, "I've devoted ten years of my life to this company. I don't want to walk away now." But the only thing worse than investing ten years into something unhealthy or unproductive is investing ten years and one day.

Impulsivity is another reason people repeat mistakes. Although there's a lot to be said for "dusting yourself off and getting right back up on the horse," it is wiser to figure out why you fell off in the first place before you try again.

Find yourself stuck in a state of perpetually repeating mistakes? You might be getting too comfortable. A woman may enter into one bad relationship after another because it's all she knows. She may keep dating men all within the same social circle who have similar problems because she lacks the confidence to look for a better prospect elsewhere. Similarly, a man may keep turning to alcohol when he feels stressed because he doesn't know how to cope with problems sober. To avoid those mistakes and do some-thing different would feel uncomfortable.

And then there are those individuals who feel so uncomfortable with success that they sabotage their own efforts. When things are going well, they may feel anxious while waiting "for the other shoe to drop." To relieve that anxiety, they resort to their old self-destructive behavior and repeat the same mistakes.

THE PROBLEM WITH REPEATING OUR MISTAKES

Kristy recognized that yelling at her kids every day wasn't helpful. She wasn't teaching them how to solve problems effectively, and they were learning that yelling was acceptable behavior. The more she yelled at them, the more they yelled right back at her. Have you ever watched a dog chase its tail around and around in a circle? That's what you feel like when you repeat your mistakes. You'll tire out, yet you won't get anywhere.

Julie came to see me for therapy because she was mad at herself. She had lost forty pounds last year but then slowly, over the last six months, she gained it all back. This wasn't the first time this had happened. She'd been gaining and losing the same forty pounds for almost a decade. She was extremely frustrated that she devoted so much time and energy into losing weight only to keep gaining it right back.

Every time she lost the weight she relaxed a little. She'd allow herself to have a second helping with dinner or she'd celebrate with ice cream. She'd find an excuse to skip a few workouts and before she knew it, she was gaining weight again. She'd quickly grown disgusted with herself and she wondered, "How can I not be in control of what I do to my own body?" Julie's story certainly isn't unique. In fact, statistically, the vast majority of people who lose weight gain it back again. Losing weight is hard work. So why would anyone go through the pain of losing it just to gain it all back? Often, it's because people begin repeating the same mistakes that caused them to become overweight in the first place.

Repeating the same mistakes leads to many problems, such as the following:

- *You won't reach your goals.* Whether you're trying to lose weight for the fifth time or you're working on quitting smoking for the tenth time, if you keep repeating the same mistakes, you won't ever reach your goals. Instead, you'll stay stuck at the same point and won't be able to move forward.

- *The problem won't get solved.* It's a vicious cycle. When you repeat a mistake, the problem perpetuates and you're more likely to just keep doing the same thing. You'll never be able to solve a problem until you do something differently.

- *You'll think differently about yourself.* You may begin to view yourself as incompetent or a complete failure be-cause you can't get past a certain obstacle.

- *You may not try as hard.* If the first few attempts weren't successful, you may be more likely to give up. When you don't try as hard, you're less likely to succeed.

- *You may frustrate others who watch you repeat the same mis-takes.* If you're guilty of always getting yourself caught up in similar problems, your friends and family may grow tired of hearing you complain. Worse yet, if they've had to bail you out because you've repeatedly gotten your-self into problematic situations, your repeated mistakes will damage your relationships.

- *You may develop irrational beliefs to excuse your mistakes.* Instead of looking at how your behavior is interfering with your progress, you may conclude it's just not "meant to be." An overweight person who struggles to lose weight and keep it off may simply decide, "I'm big-boned. I wasn't meant to be smaller."

AVOID MAKING THE SAME BLUNDERS OVER AND OVER AGAIN

To break the yelling cycle Kristy found herself stuck in, she first had to examine her discipline style and then come up with alternative consequences. She knew that in the beginning, her kids would likely test the new restrictions she imposed, so it wasn't until she developed a solid plan to deal with her emotions that she could effectively manage their misbehavior without losing her cool.

STUDY THE MISTAKE

In the mid-1800s, Rowland Macy opened a dry goods store in Haverhill, Massachusetts. Even though he opened the store in a quiet part of town that rarely attracted visitors, let alone customers, he was certain that his store would draw attention. But he was wrong and he was soon struggling to keep the doors open. In an attempt to attract business to his part of town, he arranged for a large parade, complete with a marching band, to lure people into the streets. The parade ended in front of the store where a well-known businessman from Boston was scheduled to give a speech.

Unfortunately, due to extremely hot weather on the day of the parade, no one ventured outdoors to follow the band as Rowland had expected. His marketing mistakes cost him a lot of money and, ultimately, his business.

However, Rowland was someone who learned from his mistakes and just a few short years later, he opened "R.H. Macy Dry Goods" in downtown New York. This was his fifth store, following his previous four failed businesses. But from each mistake he made, he learned something new. And by the time he opened "R.H. Macy Dry Goods," he had learned a lot about running a business and marketing it successfully.

Macy's Department Store has gone on to become one of the most successful stores in the world. Unlike Rowland's first parade, which was held during the high heat of summer, the store now carries out its annual parade, the Macy's Thanksgiving Day Parade during the cool fall weather. Not only does it attract large crowds into the streets, but it's also broadcast on TV to more than forty-four million viewers each year.

Rowland Macy didn't simply look for excuses about why his first business ventures weren't successful. Instead, he studied the facts and took responsibility for his part in each mistake. Then he was able to apply that knowledge to help him do something different the next time.

If you want to avoid repeating a mistake, spend some time studying it. Set any negative feelings you might have aside, acknowledge the factors that led up to your misstep, and learn from it. Look for an explanation without making an excuse. Ask yourself the following questions:

- *What went wrong?* Spend a little bit of time reflecting on your mistakes. Try to discern the facts about what happened. Maybe you overspend on your budget every month because you can't resist shopping. Or maybe you get into the same argument with your spouse repeatedly because the issue never really resolves itself. Examine what thoughts, behaviors, and external factors contributed to the mistake.

- *What could I have done better?* As you reflect on the situation, look for things you could have done better. Maybe you didn't stick with something long enough. For example, maybe you gave up on trying to lose weight after only two weeks. Or maybe your mistake is that you find too many excuses about why you shouldn't exercise and as a result, you just don't stick with an effective weight-loss routine. Give yourself an honest evaluation.

- *What can I do differently next time?* Saying you're not going to make a mistake again and actually doing it are two very separate things. Think about what you can do differently next time to avoid making the same mistake. Identify clear strategies you can use to avoid resorting to your old behavior.

CREATE A PLAN

During my college internship, I spent some time working in an inpatient drug and alcohol rehabilitation center. Many of the patients attending the program had tried to address their substance abuse issues before. By the time they came to our facility, they were discouraged and fed up with the fact they couldn't stop drinking and using drugs. But after a few weeks of intensive treatment, their attitudes usually shifted. They became hopeful about the future and determined that this time, they weren't going to go back to their old ways.

But, before patients could graduate from the program, they

needed a clear discharge plan. This plan was meant to help them keep the same positive outlook on recovery after they were discharged from the facility. To avoid returning to their previous habits, they needed to make some serious lifestyle changes.

For most people, that meant they had to find a new social circle. They couldn't go back to hanging around their old friends who used drugs or drank heavily. Some of them had to make job changes too. Developing healthier habits may mean ending an unhealthy relationship or trading parties for support group meetings.

Each person participated in developing a written plan that included resources and strategies to remain sober. The people who were most successful in their recovery followed their plans. Those who went back to their old lifestyles tended to relapse because they couldn't resist making the same mistakes. There were just too many unhealthy temptations when they returned to their previous environments. No matter what type of mistakes you're trying to avoid, the key to success lies in developing a good plan. Developing a written plan increases the likelihood that you'll follow through with it.

Follow these steps to create a written plan that will help you avoid repeating your mistakes:

1. *Establish behavior that will replace previous behavior.* Instead of drinking alcohol to cope with stress, a person could identify alternative strategies, such as going for a walk or calling a friend. Decide what healthy behavior will help you avoid repeating unhealthy behavior.

2. *Identify warning signs that you're headed down the wrong path again.* It's important to be on the lookout for old behavior patterns that may return. Perhaps you'll know your spending habits are getting out of control again when you begin putting purchases on credit cards.

3. *Find a way to hold yourself accountable.* It'll be more diffi-
    cult to hide your mistakes or ignore them when you're
    being held accountable. Talking to a trusted friend or
    relative who is willing to hold you accountable and
    point out your blunders can be helpful. You may also be
    able to increase the likelihood that you'll hold yourself
    accountable by keeping a journal or using a calendar to
    chart your progress.

PRACTICE SELF-DISCIPLINE

Self-discipline isn't something you either have or you don't. Instead, everyone has the ability to increase their self-discipline.
Saying no to a bag of chips or a couple of cookies requires self-
control. As does exercising when you don't feel like it. Avoiding
those mistakes that can derail your progress requires constant vigilance and hard work.

Here are some things to keep in mind when working to increase your self-control:

*   *Practice tolerating discomfort.* Whether you're feeling lonely
    and you're tempted to text message that ex who isn't
    good for you or you're craving a sweet treat that will
    blow your diet, practice tolerating the discomfort. Al-
    though people often convince themselves if they "give
    in just this once" it will help, research shows otherwise.
    Each time you give in you reduce your self-control.

*   *Use positive self-talk.* Realistic affirmations can help you
    resist temptation in moments of weakness. Saying things
    like "I can do this" or "I'm doing a great job working
    toward my goals" can help you stay on track.

- *Keep your goals in mind.* Focusing on the importance of your goals helps decrease temptations. So if you focus on how good you'll feel when your car is paid off, you'll be less tempted to make that purchase that will wreak havoc on the month's budget.

- *Impose restrictions on yourself.* If you know you're likely to spend too much money when you're out with friends, only take a small amount of cash with you. Take steps that make it difficult, if not impossible, for you to give in when you're faced with temptation.

- *Create a list of all the reasons why you don't want to repeat your mistake.* Carry this list with you. When you're tempted to resort to your previous behavior pattern, read this list to yourself. It can increase your motivation to resist repeating old patterns. For example, create a list of reasons why you should go for a walk after dinner. When you're tempted to watch TV instead of exercise, read the list and it may increase your motivation to move forward.

LEARNING FROM MISTAKES WILL MAKE YOU STRONGER

After quitting school at the age of twelve, Milton Hershey went to work at a print shop, but he soon realized he wasn't interested in a career in the printing business. So he went to work at a candy and ice cream shop. At the age of nineteen, he decided to open his own candy company. He gained financial support from his family and got the business off the ground. However, the company wasn't successful and within a few years, he was forced to declare bankruptcy.

Following his failed business attempt, he went to Colorado where he hoped to get rich in the booming silver mining industry. But he arrived too late and he struggled to find work. He eventually found a job with another candy maker. It was there that he learned how fresh milk made excellent candy.

Hershey moved to New York City to open his own candy business again. He hoped the skills and information he had learned would help his second candy venture become a success. But Hershey lacked funding, and there were too many other candy stores in the area. Again, his endeavor failed. At this point, many people in his family who had helped fund his entrepreneurial efforts shunned him for his mistakes.

But Hershey didn't give up. He moved back to Pennsylvania and opened a caramel-making company. He made candy during the day and sold caramels on the streets during the evenings with a pushcart. He eventually received a large order and was able to secure a bank loan to fill it. As soon as the order was paid for, Hershey was able to pay off the loan and launch the Lancaster Caramel Company. Soon, he became a millionaire and one of the most successful businesspeople in his area.

He continued to expand his business. He began making chocolate, and by 1900, he sold the Lancaster Caramel Company and opened a chocolate factory. Hershey worked tirelessly on perfecting his chocolate formula. He quickly became the only person in the United States to mass-produce milk chocolate, and soon he began selling chocolate all over the world.

When sugar became scarce during World War I, Hershey established his own sugar refinery in Cuba. But as soon as the war ended, the sugar market collapsed. Once again, Hershey found himself in financial trouble. He borrowed money from the bank, but he had to mortgage his properties until the loan was paid off. Nevertheless, Hershey managed to get his business back in order and he paid off the loan within two years.

Not only did he build a thriving chocolate factory, but he created a thriving town. During the Great Depression, Hershey was able to keep his employees working. He created a variety of buildings in the town, including a school, a sports arena, and a hotel. The new construction employed many people. Throughout all his success, he also became a great philanthropist. Hershey's ability to learn from his mistakes helped him go from running failed candy businesses to owning the world's biggest chocolate company. Even today, the town known as Hershey, Pennsylvania, is adorned with streetlights in the shape of Hershey's Kisses, and over three million visitors tour the Hershey's world chocolate factory to learn how Milton Hershey made chocolate go from a bean to a bar.

When you view mistakes not as something negative but instead as an opportunity to improve yourself, you'll be able to devote time and energy into making sure you don't repeat them. In fact, mentally strong people are often willing to share their mistakes with other people in an effort to help prevent them from making the same mistakes.

In the case of Kristy, she felt enormous relief once she was able to stop yelling at her children every day. She learned that it was normal for her kids to break the rules at times, but she had choices in how she responded. She felt like their home was a much happier place when they weren't yelling at one another. When Kristy stopped repeating her discipline mistakes and was able to impose effective consequences for her kids, she felt more in control of herself and of her life.

TROUBLESHOOTING AND COMMON TRAPS

There are usually many different ways to solve a particular problem. If your current method hasn't been successful, be open to trying something new. Learning from each mistake requires self-awareness and humility, but it can be one of the biggest keys to reaching your full potential.

WHAT'S HELPFUL

Acknowledging your personal responsibility for each mistake

Creating a written plan to prevent repeating the mistake

Identifying triggers and warning signs of old behavior patterns

Practicing self-discipline strategies

WHAT'S NOT HELPFUL

Making excuses or refusing to examine your role in the outcome

Responding impulsively without thinking about alternatives

Putting yourself in situations where you are likely to fail

Assuming you can always resist temptation or deciding you're doomed to keep repeating your mistakes

CHAPTER 9

THEY DON'T RESENT OTHER PEOPLE'S SUCCESS

Resentment is like drinking poison and then hoping it will kill your enemies.
—NELSON MANDELA

Dan and his family frequently attended social gatherings in their neighborhood. They lived in the type of community where backyard barbecues were common and parents often attended each other's children's birthday parties. Dan and his wife even hosted get-togethers on occasion. From all accounts, Dan was a friendly, outgoing man who seemed to have it all together. He had a nice house and a good job with a reputable company. He also had a lovely wife and two healthy children. But Dan had a secret.

He despised attending parties where he had to hear about Michael's impressive promotion or Bill's brand-new car. It angered Dan that his neighbors could afford expensive vacations and the greatest toys on the market. Ever since he and his wife had decided that she should quit her job to become a stay-at-home parent a few years ago, money was tight. His efforts to keep up the appearance of financial abundance had left Dan deeply in debt. In fact, he was keeping secrets from his wife about the extent *of their financial problems. But Dan felt he needed to keep up the charade that they could financially compete with the neighbors, at all costs.*

Dan decided to seek help when his wife told him he needed to do something about his short fuse. When he initially came to therapy, he said he wasn't sure how therapy could help. He knew his irritability was caused by the fact that he was so tired all the time. And the reason he was so tired was because he had to work long hours to pay the bills.

We talked about his financial situation and the reasons he felt compelled to work such long hours. At first, he blamed his neighbors for his long workdays. He said they all prided themselves on having such nice things that he was forced to keep up with them. When I gently challenged whether he was "forced" to keep up with them, he agreed that he didn't have to, but he wanted to.

Dan agreed to attend a few more therapy sessions, and over the next few weeks his resentment toward his neighbors became apparent. When we explored some of the reasons why he was so angry with his neighbors, Dan revealed that he had grown up poor and he never wanted his children to feel like he did as a child. He'd been teased and bullied because his family couldn't afford expensive clothing or toys like the other kids had. So he prided himself on keeping up with other people so he could offer his family a comparable lifestyle to those around him.

Deep down, however, Dan valued time with his family more than his possessions. And the more we talked about the type of lifestyle he was living, the more disgusted he felt with himself. He knew he'd rather spend time with his family than work overtime to buy them more things. Slowly, Dan began to change the way he thought about his behavior, and he focused more on his own goals and his own values, rather than keeping up with the neighbors.

Dan's wife eventually joined him for a therapy session, and he revealed to her that he'd been borrowing money at times to pay the bills. She was understandably surprised to hear Dan's confession, but he shared with her his new plan to live according to his values, and not above their means just to compete with the neighbors. She became supportive of him and agreed to hold him accountable throughout the process.

It took a lot of work for Dan to change the way he thought about himself, his neighbors, and his overall status in his life. But once he stopped competing with his neighbors and he began focusing on the things that were really important to him, he felt a lot less resentment toward others. He also became a lot less irritable.

GREEN WITH ENVY

While jealousy can be described as "I want what you have," resentment over someone's success goes further: "I want what you have and I don't want you to have it." Fleeting and occasional jealousy is normal. But resentment is unhealthy. Do any of these statements sound familiar?

- ☐ You often compare your wealth, status, and appearance to the people around you.

- ☐ You feel envious of people who can afford nicer possessions than you can.

- ☐ It's difficult for you to listen to other people share their success stories.

- ☐ You think you deserve more recognition for your accomplishments than you actually receive.

- ☐ You worry that other people perceive you as a loser.

- ☐ It sometimes feels like no matter how hard you try, everyone else seems to be more successful.

- ☐ You feel disgust, rather than joy, toward people who are able to achieve their dreams.

☐ It's hard to be around people who make more money than you do.

☐ You feel embarrassed by your lack of success.

☐ You sometimes imply to others that you're doing better than you actually are.

☐ You secretly experience joy when a successful person encounters misfortune.

If you feel resentment over someone else's accomplishments, it's likely based on irrational thinking and can cause you to begin behaving in an illogical manner. Take steps to focus on your own path to success without resenting anyone else's prosperity.

WHY WE RESENT OTHER PEOPLE'S SUCCESS

Although feelings of resentment are similar to those of anger, when someone feels angry, they are more likely to express themselves. Resentment, however, usually remains hidden, and people like Dan mask their true feelings with feigned kindness. Yet beneath the smile is a seething mixture of indignation and envy.

Dan's resentment stemmed from a sense of injustice. Sometimes an injustice is real, and at other times, it's imagined. Dan felt it wasn't fair that his neighbors were making a lot of money. He was fixated on the fact that they had more money and nicer possessions than he could afford. He blamed his neighbors for making him feel poor, but had he lived in a less affluent neighborhood, he may have felt rich.

Resentment of others' success is also a result of deep-rooted insecurities. It's hard to be happy about a friend's accomplishments when you feel bad about yourself. When you're insecure, someone else's success will seem to magnify your shortcomings. You might also become bitter when you wrongfully assume that good fortune comes more easily to others when you're the more deserving one.

It's easy to resent what others have when you don't even know what you want yourself. Someone who never wanted a job that requires travel may look at a friend who goes on international business trips and think, *She's so lucky. I want to do that.* Meanwhile, he may also covet the lifestyle of another friend who operates a home-based business that prevents him from traveling and think, *I wish I could do that,* even though these two lifestyles are conflicting. You can't have everything you want.

When you overlook the fact that most people only reach their goals by investing time, money, and effort to get there, it's more likely that you'll resent their achievements. It's easy to look at a professional athlete and say, "I wish I could do that." But do you really? Do you wish you got up and worked out twelve hours a day? Do you really wish your entire income rested solely upon your athletic abilities that will decline as you age? Do you really wish you could give up eating the foods you love so you can stay in shape? Do you really wish you could give up spending time with friends and family to keep practicing your game year-round?

THE PROBLEM WITH RESENTING OTHER PEOPLE'S SUCCESS

Dan's resentment toward his neighbors affected almost every area of his life—his career, his spending habits, and even his relationship with his wife. It consumed him to the point that it interfered with his mood and prevented him from enjoying social gatherings in the neighborhood. And he was setting himself up for a vicious cycle—the more effort he put into trying to compete with his neighbors' success, the more resentment he felt toward them.

YOUR VIEW OF OTHER PEOPLE ISN'T ACCURATE

You never actually know what goes on behind closed doors. Dan had no idea what type of problems his neighbors may have actually been experiencing. But he resented them based on what he saw.

Feelings of resentment can crop up based on a stereotype alone. Perhaps you believe "rich" people are evil or maybe you think "business owners" are greedy. Those types of stereotypes can lead you to resent someone without even knowing them.

A 2013 study titled "Their Pain, Our Pleasure: Stereotype Content and Schadenfreude" revealed that people not only resented "a rich professional's" success, but participants went so far as to take joy in that person's misfortune. Researchers showed participants photographs of four different people—an elderly person, a student, a drug addict, and a rich professional. They studied participants' brain activities while pairing the images with various events. They discovered that the participants showed the most glee when the rich professional experienced problems, like getting soaked by a taxi. In fact, people enjoyed that scenario even more than scenarios where any of the individuals received good fortune. And it was all based on the stereotype that somehow "rich professionals are bad."

Resentment can easily consume your entire life if you're not careful. Here are some of the problems that it can cause:

- *You'll stop focusing on your own path to success.* The more time you spend focusing on someone else's achievements, the less time you have to work on your own goals. Animosity over someone else's achievements only serves as a distraction that will slow down your progress.

- *You'll never be content with what you have.* If you're always trying to keep up with other people, you'll never feel a sense of peace with what you have. You'll spend your whole life continually trying to get ahead of everyone else. You'll never be satisfied because there will always be someone who has more money, who is more attractive, and who appears to have everything all together.

- *You'll overlook your skills and talents.* The more time you spend wishing you could do what someone else does, the less time you'll focus on sharpening your own skills. Wishing that other people lacked talent won't improve your talent.

- *You may abandon your values.* Resentment can cause people to behave in a desperate manner. It's hard to stay true to your values when you feel a lot of anger toward people who have things you don't. Unfortunately, resentment can lead people to behave in a manner they normally wouldn't— like sabotage someone else's efforts or go into debt to try and keep up.

- *You may damage relationships.* When you resent someone, you won't be able to maintain a healthy relationship with him or her. Resentment leads to indirect communication, sarcasm, and irritability that is often hidden under a fake smile. You won't be able to have an authentic and genuine relationship with someone when you're holding secret grudges.

- *You may begin tooting your own horn.* At first, you may copy someone you resent in an effort to keep up. But if that person's accomplishments seem to be overshadowing yours, you may resort to boasting about yourself or even outright lying about your accomplishments. Attempts to "outdo" or "one-up" other people usually aren't flattering, but sometimes, resentful people behave this way out of desperation to try and prove their worth.

CURB YOUR JEALOUSY

Dan had to pause to evaluate his own life before he could stop resenting other people for their achievements. Once he chose to create his own definition of success—which involved spending time with his family and raising his children according to his values—he was able to remind himself that his neighbors' good fortune didn't diminish his efforts to reach his goals.

In addition to addressing his insecurities, Dan had to challenge his thinking. He had convinced himself that if he didn't give his children the best clothing and the latest technological gadgets like all the other kids in the neighborhood had, they'd get bullied. Once he began to recognize that almost all kids get teased sometimes, and that there were no guarantees that material possessions would prevent that, he was able to stop perseverating on his need to buy them everything. When it hit him that he might unintentionally be causing them to become materialistic, which wasn't a characteristic he wanted them to have, he turned his efforts to spending quality time with them.

CHANGE YOUR CIRCUMSTANCES

I had been working with a man in my therapy office for a couple of months who was battling a lot of different issues. He yelled at his kids and swore at his wife daily. He smoked marijuana a couple of times a day and drank to the point of passing out a few times a week. He had been "in between jobs" for over six months and he was way behind on his bills. He routinely complained about how unfair his life was, and he constantly argued with anyone who offered him help. One day, he entered my office and said, "Amy, I don't feel good about myself." To his horror, I said, "That's good." He looked perplexed as he said, "Why would you say that? Your job is to help me with my self-esteem." I explained to him that based on his current behavior, not feeling good about himself was actually a healthy sign. The last thing I wanted to do was help him feel good about himself in his present situation. Of course I wouldn't have said that so blatantly to just anyone, but I'd known him for a while and I had a good enough rapport with him that I knew he'd be able to tolerate hearing it.

Over the next few months I had the pleasure of watching him grow and change. And by the end of treatment, he felt better about himself, but not simply because he repeatedly showered himself with false accolades. Instead, he gained an income, quit abusing drugs and alcohol, and worked hard on treating people with kindness. His marriage improved. His relationship with his daughters improved. He felt much better once he began behaving according to his values. Feeling bad was an indicator that he needed to change.

If you don't feel good about who you are, it's important to examine what the reason might be. Perhaps you aren't behaving in a way that builds healthy self-worth. If that's the case, examine what you can do differently in your life to bring your behavior in line with your values and your goals.

CHANGE YOUR ATTITUDE

If you're already behaving in the manner that aligns with your values and goals, yet you still resent other people's accomplishments, there may be some irrational thoughts interfering with your ability to appreciate their successes. If you're constantly thinking things like *I'm stupid* or *I'm not as good as other people,* it's likely that you'll feel resentment when you see other people enjoying success. Not only might you be thinking irrationally about yourself, but you may also have irrational thoughts about other people.

A 2013 study titled "Envy on Facebook: A Hidden Threat to Users' Life Satisfaction" explains why some people experience negative emotions while browsing Facebook. Researchers discovered that people felt the most anger and resentment when their "friends" shared vacation photos. They also experienced resentment when their "friends" received a lot of "Happy Birthday" wishes on their birthdays. Frighteningly, the study concluded that those who experience a lot of negative emotions while browsing Facebook experience an overall decline in general life satisfaction. Is that really what this world has come to—that we become dissatisfied with our own lives if we think another grown adult received a lot of birthday wishes on Facebook? Or that we feel resentful because our friend went away on a vacation?

If you find yourself resenting other people, use these strategies to change your thoughts:

- *Avoid comparing yourself to other people.* Comparing yourself to others is like comparing apples and oranges. You have your own set of unique talents, skills, and life experiences, so comparing yourself to other people isn't an accurate way to measure your self-worth. Instead, compare yourself to who you used to be and measure how you're growing as an individual.

- *Develop an awareness of your stereotypes.* Work on getting to know people instead of automatically judging them based on stereotypes. Don't allow yourself to assume that someone who has gained wealth, fame, or whatever else you may envy is somehow evil.

- *Stop emphasizing your weaknesses.* If you focus on all the things you don't have or can't do, you may set yourself up to resent the people who do possess those things. Focus on your strengths, skills, and abilities.

- *Quit magnifying other people's strengths.* Resentment often derives from exaggerating how great other people are doing and focusing on everything that they have. Remember that each person also has weaknesses, insecurities, and problems—even those who are successful.

- *Don't insult other people's accomplishments.* Diminishing someone else's accomplishments will only breed feelings of resentment. Avoid saying things like "His promotion actually wasn't a big deal. And he only got it because he's friends with the boss."

- *Stop trying to determine what's fair.* Don't allow yourself to focus on things that aren't fair. Unfortunately, sometimes people cheat to get ahead. And some people may become successful simply based on chance. But the more time you devote to thinking about who is "deserving" of success and who isn't, the less time you'll have to devote to something productive.

FOCUS ON COOPERATION RATHER THAN COMPETITION

In my practice I've met with many married couples who keep score and demand that things be "fair." I've also seen bosses who resent their own employees' success, even when it benefits their company.

As long as you view the people in your life as competitors, you'll always focus on trying to "win." And you can't have healthy relationships with people when you're only thinking about how to beat them, rather than build them up. Spend some time examining those in your life whom you view as your competition. Perhaps you want to be more attractive than your best friend. Or you want to have more money than your brother. Take notice of how viewing these people as your competition really isn't healthy to your relationship. What if, instead, you began to view them as on your team? Including people in your life who possess a variety of skills and talents can actually work to your advantage. If you've got a brother who is good with money, instead of trying to buy just as many expensive toys as he has, why not learn from his financial tips? If you've got a neighbor who is health conscious, why not ask her to share some recipes? Behaving in a humble manner can do wonders for how you feel about yourself, as well as other people.

As we learned a chapter ago, some of Milton Hershey's success was based on the fact that he learned from his mistakes, but his ability to accept the success of others also helped him along the way. He didn't even become resentful when one of his employees, H. B. Reese, began another candy company in the same town. While still working in the chocolate factory, Reese used the knowledge he'd gained from Hershey to invent his own candy. After a few years, Reese created chocolate-covered peanut butter cups and he used the Hershey chocolate factory as his supplier of milk chocolate.

Although Hershey could have easily viewed Reese as a competitor who was stealing customers away from his chocolate business, he instead supported Reese's business ventures. The two remained on good terms while both were selling candy in the same community. In fact, after both their deaths, the Hershey Chocolate Corporation and the Reese Candy Company merged, and Reese's peanut butter cups remain one of Hershey's most popular products today. Clearly, the story could have ended quite differently. In fact, it may have ruined both their businesses had they not cooperated. But instead, the two men remained friendly and cooperative throughout their careers.

When you're able to be happy about other people's accomplishments, you'll attract—rather than repel—successful people. Surrounding yourself with others who are working hard to reach their goals can be good for you. You may gain motivation, inspiration, and information that can help you along your journey.

CREATE YOUR OWN DEFINITION OF SUCCESS

Although many people equate success with money, clearly not everyone desires to be wealthy. Maybe your definition of success in life is being able to give back to the community by donating your time and skills. Perhaps you'll feel best about yourself when you work fewer hours and you're able to offer your time to people in need. If that's your definition of success, there's no need to resent someone who chooses to earn a lot of money because that's consistent with his or her definition of success.

When people say, "I have everything I ever wanted, but I'm still not happy," it's often because they don't really have everything they ever wanted. They're living according to someone else's definition of success instead of being true to themselves. Take the case of Dan. He was working to have all the same material possessions his neighbors had. Yet that wasn't making him happy. Instead, he and his wife had chosen for her to be a stay-at-home parent because that was more important to them than the extra money she would have earned while working. But he lost sight of his values and began copying his neighbors.

To create your own definition of success, sometimes it's best to look at the big picture of your life and not just the phase that you're in right now. Imagine being at the end of your life looking back over the years. What answers to these questions would likely give you the biggest sense of peace?

- *What were my biggest accomplishments in life?* Would your biggest accomplishments likely involve money? The contributions you made to other people? The family that you built? The business you created? The fact you made a difference in the world?

- *How would I know that I had accomplished those things?* What evidence do you have that demonstrates you reached your goals? Did people tell you they appreciated your contributions? Do you have a bank account to prove you made plenty of money?

- *What were the best ways I spent my time, money, and talents?* Which memories in your life will likely be the most important to you? What types of activities will give you the most sense of pride and fulfillment?

Write down your definition of success. When you're tempted to resent other individuals who are working toward their own definitions of success, remind yourself of your definition. Everyone's path to success is different and it's important to recognize that your journey is unique.

PRACTICE CELEBRATING OTHER PEOPLE'S ACCOMPLISHMENTS

If you're working toward your own definition of success and you've addressed your insecurities, you can celebrate other people's accomplishments without any feelings of resentment. You'll stop worrying that someone else's success will make you look bad once you accept that you aren't in direct competition. Instead, you'll genuinely feel happy for someone who reaches a new milestone, earns more money, or does something you haven't done.

Peter Bookman is an excellent example of someone who celebrates other people's accomplishments, even though by some accounts, he should feel resentful. As a self-described serial entrepreneur, he's been involved in creating a variety of successful start-up companies. He was the founder of the company that eventually became Fusion-io, a computer hardware and software systems company whose client list includes companies like Facebook and Apple. After three and a half years helping to build the business, Peter was told the investors and board of directors had a different vision for the future than he had. So Peter left the company and watched many of the people he had hired go on to become very successful.

In fact, Fusion-io went on to become a billion-dollar business, earning the founders $250 million after Peter left. Rather than resenting his former company's success, Peter feels happy for them. He acknowledges that a lot of people have told him he should be angry about how the company he started went on to be so successful without him. When I asked him why he doesn't harbor any animosity he said, "I don't see how their success robs me of anything. I am happy to have played my part and look forward to helping others achieve their dreams regardless of whether the outcome ends up in my best interest or not." Peter clearly isn't wasting a minute of his life resenting anyone's success. He's too busy celebrating alongside people when they reach their dreams.

HOW EMBRACING THE ACCOMPLISHMENTS OF OTHERS WILL MAKE YOU STRONGER

By all accounts, Herb Brooks had been a successful hockey player throughout both high school and college, and in 1960, he became a member of the U.S. Olympic hockey team. One week before the Olympic Games began, however, Brooks became the last person cut from the team. He was left to watch his former teammates go on without him and win the first men's hockey gold medal in U.S. history. Instead of expressing anger at being cut from the winning team, Brooks approached the coach and said, "Well, you must have made the right decision—you won."

Although many people may have been tempted to quit playing hockey altogether, Brooks wasn't ready to give up. He continued on to play in the 1964 and 1968 Olympic Games. His teams never reached the same level of success as the year in which he was cut from the team, but his hockey career didn't end there. Once he retired as a player, he went on to be a coach.

After coaching at the collegiate level for several years, he was hired to coach the Olympic team. When choosing players for his team, he looked for players who could work together well. He didn't want any one player attempting to steal the spotlight. Brooks's team entered the 1980 Olympics as underdogs, while the Soviet Union national team had won the gold medal six out of the last seven Olympic Games. But with Brooks's coaching, the United States beat the Soviets 4–3. Their stunning upset became known as the "Miracle on Ice." From there, they went on to defeat Finland and took the gold medal.

Herb left the ice as soon as his team won and he disappeared from the cameras. He was known for taking off right after the game rather than staying to celebrate the team's victories. He later told reporters he wanted to leave the ice to his players, who deserved it. He didn't want to steal their spotlight.

Not only did Herb Brooks not resent those who were successful, but he also supported them in their efforts. He didn't want to force anyone to share their success with him, but instead, was humbly willing to give others all the glory. "Write your own book instead of reading someone else's book about success," he famously told his players.

When you stop resenting people for their success, you'll be free to work toward your own goals. You'll have the desire to live according to your own values and you won't feel offended or cheated by people living according to theirs.

Dan felt a sense of peace and liberation as soon as he began focusing on reaching his own definition of success. Rather than compete with his neighbors, he began competing with himself. He wanted to challenge himself to be a little better each day. Just like in the case of Dan, living an authentic lifestyle is essential to anyone who wants true success in life.

TROUBLESHOOTING AND COMMON TRAPS

Sometimes it's easy to avoid feeling resentful of others when you're doing really well. But there will likely be times in life where you're going to struggle. That's when it can be most difficult to not resent other people. It takes hard work and persistence to keep your feelings in check when you're struggling to reach your goals while those around you are reaching theirs.

WHAT'S HELPFUL

Creating your own definition of success

Replacing negative thoughts that breed resentment with more rational thoughts

Celebrating other people's accomplishments

Focusing on your strengths

Cooperating rather than competing with everyone

WHAT'S NOT HELPFUL

Chasing after everyone else's dreams

Imagining how much better everyone else's lives are

Constantly comparing yourself to everyone around you

Diminishing other people's achievements

Treating everyone like they're your direct competition

CHAPTER 10

THEY DON'T GIVE UP AFTER THE FIRST FAILURE

Failure is part of the process of success. People who avoid
failure also avoid success.
—ROBERT T. KIYOSAKI

Susan came to see me for counseling because she said she felt like her life
wasn't as fulfilling as she thought it should be. She was happily married
and she and her husband had a beautiful two-year-old little girl. Susan had
a stable job as a receptionist at the local school and she and her husband
were doing just fine financially. Susan said she actually felt a little selfish
for not feeling happier, because she knew she had a good life.

During the first couple of therapy sessions, Susan revealed that she had
always wanted to be a teacher. After high school, she'd actually gone on
to study education in college. Even though the university she had attended
was only a few hours away from home, she was miserably homesick. She
was painfully shy and she struggled to make new friends. She found the
classes to be difficult and overwhelming. So, halfway through her first se-
mester, Susan dropped out of college.

Shortly after returning home, she got the school receptionist job and she'd worked there ever since. Although it wasn't her dream job, she thought it was as close to becoming a teacher as she'd ever get. But it was clear from talking to Susan that she still yearned to be a teacher. She just didn't have the confidence that she could do it.

When I first broached the subject of going back to college, Susan insisted she was too old. But she changed her mind when I showed her a recent news headline about a woman who earned her high school diploma at the age of ninety-four. We spent the next few weeks talking about what held her back from studying education. She said that she had simply decided that she wasn't "college material." After all, she'd failed the first time and she felt certain she wasn't smart enough to pass college classes now that she'd been out of school for so long.

Over the next few weeks, we discussed her thoughts about failure and whether it was true that if she failed once, she'd fail again. We discovered an obvious pattern in Susan's life—whenever she wasn't successful on her first attempt at anything, she gave up. When she didn't make her high school basketball team, she quit playing sports. When she gained back the fifteen pounds she'd lost dieting, she quit trying to lose weight. The list went on as she discovered how her beliefs about failure influenced her choices.

In the meantime, I encouraged her to look around at college options, even if she never planned to go to school, because college has changed a lot in the last fifteen years. She was pleased to discover that there were many alternatives to being a full-time college student, and within a matter of weeks, she signed up to take some online college classes. She was thrilled to think that classes wouldn't require much time away from her family and she could attend on a part-time basis.

Soon after she began taking classes, she announced that she felt like she'd found what was missing. Simply working toward a new professional goal seemed to be just the challenge she needed to help her feel fulfilled. She ended therapy shortly after with a new sense of hope about her future and a new outlook on failure.

IF AT FIRST YOU DON'T SUCCEED . . .

While some people are motivated by failure to do better the next time, other people simply give up. Do any of these points resonate with you?

❏ You worry about being perceived as a failure by other people.

❏ You only like to participate in things where you're likely to excel.

❏ If your first attempt at something doesn't work out well, you're not likely to try again.

❏ You believe the most successful people were born with the natural talent to succeed.

❏ There are plenty of things that you don't think you could ever learn to do, no matter how hard you try.

❏ Much of your self-worth is linked to your ability to succeed.

❏ The thought of failing feels very unsettling.

❏ You tend to make excuses for your failure.

❏ You would rather show off the skills you already have than try to learn new skills.

Failure doesn't have to be the end. In fact, most successful people treat failure as just the beginning of a long journey to success.

WHY WE GIVE UP

Susan, like many of us, felt that if she failed once, she'd most certainly fail again, so she didn't bother trying. Although she knew something was missing from her life, it never occurred to her that she could try taking college classes again because she assumed she just wasn't "college material." Susan is certainly not alone. It's likely that almost everyone has given up on something after a failed first attempt.

Fear is often at the heart of our unwillingness to try something again after we've failed at it already, but not everyone shares the same fears about failure. One person may worry that he'll disappoint his parents while another person may worry that she's too fragile to handle another setback. Rather than facing these fears, many people simply avoid risking another failure, which we associate with shame. Some of us try to hide our failures; others devote a lot of energy into making excuses for them. A student may say, "I didn't have time to study for this test at all," even though she devoted many hours of her time preparing, just to cover up the fact that she did poorly. Another student may hide his test score from his parents because he's ashamed that he didn't do well.

In other instances, we allow failure to define who we are. To Susan, her failure to finish college meant she wasn't smart enough to get an education. Someone may believe one failure in business means he was never destined to be an entrepreneur, or an individual who fails to publish his first book may conclude he's a poor writer.

Giving up can also be a learned behavior. Perhaps as a child, your mother swooped in to help you accomplish any task you weren't able to do on the first try. Or maybe when you told your teacher you couldn't figure out your math work, she gave you the answers so you never really had to figure it out for yourself. Always expecting someone else to come to our rescue can be a hard habit to break, even into adulthood, making it less likely that we'll be willing to try again if we fail.

Finally, many people give up because they have a fixed mindset about their abilities. They don't think that they have any control over their level of talent so they don't bother improving and trying again after failure. They think if you weren't born with a God-given talent to do something, there's no use in trying to learn.

THE PROBLEM WITH GIVING IN TO FAILURE

Susan spent a lot of time thinking things like *I'm not smart enough to be a teacher,* and *I could never help students succeed because I'm a failure.* Those types of thoughts kept her from achieving her goals, and it never occurred to her that she could still go back to college. If you give up like Susan did after your first failure, you will likely miss out on a lot of opportunities in your life. Failing can actually be a wonderful experience—but only if you move forward with the knowledge you gain from it.

It's difficult to succeed without failing at least once. Take, for example, Theodor Geisel—also known as Dr. Seuss—whose first book was rejected by more than twenty publishers. He eventually went on to publish forty-six of the most well-known children's books, some of which were turned into television specials, feature films, and Broadway musicals. Had he given up the first time he failed to get a publishing deal, the world would never have had the opportunity to appreciate his unique writing style that has been entertaining children for decades.

Giving up after the first failure can easily become a self-fulfilling prophecy. Each time you quit, you reinforce the idea that failure is bad, which in turn will prevent you from trying again; thus your fear of failure inhibits your ability to learn. In a 1998 study published in the *Journal of Personality and Social Psychology*, researchers compared fifth-grade children who were praised for their intelligence and children who were praised for their efforts. All the children were given a very difficult test. After they were shown their scores, they were given two options—they could look at the tests of children who scored lower or the tests of children who scored higher. The children who were praised for their intelligence were most likely to look at the scores of the children who scored lower so they could bolster their self-esteem. Children who had been praised for their efforts were more eager to look at the tests of children who scored better so they could learn from their mistakes. If you're afraid of failure, you'll be less likely to learn from mistakes and, therefore, less likely to try again.

DON'T GIVE UP

As soon as Susan realized that just because she failed once didn't necessarily mean she'd fail again, she was more open to looking at her options for an education. Once she started behaving like someone who could recover from failure—by researching colleges—she began to feel more hopeful that she could fulfill her dream of becoming a teacher.

IDENTIFY BELIEFS ABOUT FAILURE THAT PREVENT YOU FROM TRYING AGAIN

Thomas Edison was one of the most prolific inventors of all time. He held 1,093 patents for his products and the systems to support those products. Some of his most famous inventions included the electric lightbulb, motion pictures, and the phonograph. But not all his inventions became wildly successful. You've probably never heard of his electric pen or the ghost machine. Those are just a couple of his many failed inventions.

Edison knew that a certain number of his inventions were bound to fail and when he created a product that either didn't work or didn't seem to be a hit with the market, he didn't view himself as a failure. In fact, he considered each failure to be an important learning opportunity. According to a biography written about Thomas Edison in 1915, a young assistant once commented that it was a shame that they had been working for weeks without seeing any results, and Edison replied by saying, "Results! No results? Why, man, I have gotten a lot of results! I know several thousand things that won't work."

If you refuse to try again after you fail once, it's likely you have developed some inaccurate or unproductive beliefs about failure. Those beliefs influence the way you think, feel, and behave toward failure. Here's what the research says about perseverance and failure:

- *Deliberate practice is more important than natural talent.* Although we're often led to believe that we're either gifted with natural-born talent or we aren't, most talents can be cultivated through hard work. Research studies have found that after ten years of daily practice, people can surpass others with natural talent in chess, sports, music, and the visual arts. After twenty years of dedicated practice, many people who lack natural talent can gain world-class achievement. But often we believe if we weren't born with a specific gift, we won't ever be able to develop enough talent to become successful. This belief can cause you to give up before you've had a chance to cultivate the skills necessary to succeed.

- *Grit is a better predictor of success than IQ.* Clearly, not everyone with a high IQ reaches a high level of achievement. In fact, a person's IQ isn't a very good predictor of whether he or she will become successful. Grit, defined as perseverance and passion for long-term goals, has been shown to be a much more accurate predictor of achievement than IQ.

- *Attributing failure to a lack of ability leads to learned helplessness.* If you think that your failure is caused by a lack of ability—and you think you can't improve upon that ability—you're likely to develop a sense of learned helplessness. Instead of trying again after you fail, you'll either give up or wait for someone else to do it for you. If you think you can't improve, you likely won't try to get better.

Don't allow inaccurate beliefs about your abilities to hold you back from becoming successful. Spend some time thinking about your beliefs surrounding failure. Look at your path to success as a marathon and not a sprint. Accept that failure is part of the process that helps you learn and grow.

CHANGE THE WAY YOU THINK ABOUT FAILURE

If you think failure is terrible, you'll struggle to try a task over again if you've already failed at it once. Here are some thoughts about failure that will likely discourage you from trying again:

- *Failure is unacceptable.*

- *I'm either a complete success or a complete failure.*

- *Failure is always all my fault.*

- *I failed because I'm bad.*

- *People won't like me if I fail.*

- *If I couldn't do something right the first time, I won't be able to do it right the second time.*

- *I'm not good enough to succeed.*

Irrational thoughts about failure may cause you to quit after your first failed attempt. Work on replacing them with more realistic thoughts. Failure isn't likely as bad as you make it out to be in your mind. Focus on your efforts instead of the outcome. When you're trying to complete a difficult task, focus on what you could gain from the challenge. Can you learn something new? Can you improve your skills even if you aren't initially successful? By thinking about what you can learn from the experience, you'll be more likely to accept that failure is part of the process.

Self-compassion, and not necessarily high self-esteem, may be the key to reaching your full potential. While being too hard on yourself can lead to the resignation that you're just not good enough, and being too easy on yourself may lead to excuses for your behavior, self-compassion strikes just the right balance. Self-compassion means viewing your failures kindly yet realistically. It means understanding that everyone has shortcomings, including you, and that failure doesn't decrease your worth as a person. When you take a compassionate approach to your own weaknesses, you'll be more likely to recognize there is room to grow and improve.

In a 2012 study titled "Self-Compassion Increased Self-Improvement Motivation," students were given a chance to improve failed test scores. One group of students took a self-compassionate view of their failure while the other group focused on bolstering their self-esteem. The results found that the students who practiced self-compassion studied 25 percent longer and scored higher on the second test compared with the students who focused on increasing their self-esteem.

Avoid making your entire self-worth contingent upon high achievement or you'll be less likely to risk doing things where you may fail. Replace the irrational thoughts with these realistic reminders:

- *Failure is often part of the journey to success.*

- *I can handle failure.*

- *I can learn from my failures.*

- *Failure is a sign that I'm challenging myself and I can choose to try again.*

- *I have the power to overcome failure if I choose.*

FACE YOUR FEAR OF FAILURE

My father-in-law, Rob, was the type of guy who could always laugh at himself and he felt no shame in repeating his stories about failure to everyone. But I don't think he considered any of them failures. In fact, I'm pretty certain that if it made for a good story, he considered his adventure a success.

One story that stands out in my mind stems back from his days as a pilot in the 1960s. He used to fly people around on private aircraft as an air taxi service. Sometimes he picked up customers who were getting off a commercial flight and were then taking an air taxi to their final destination. One particular time he was picking up a wealthy businessman. Since airport security was a lot more relaxed back then, he was able to greet the man right when he stepped off his commercial plane onto the tarmac.

While most private pilots would have waited, holding a sign that read their customer's name, that wasn't Rob's style. Instead, when his passenger stepped off the plane, Rob shook his hand and said, "Great to meet you, Mr. Smith. I'll be your pilot today." Mr. Smith responded by saying how flattered he was that Rob recognized him right away. But what Mr. Smith didn't know was that Rob had actually shaken every man's hand as he stepped off the plane and uttered the exact same words, "Great to meet you, Mr. Smith." If the person looked confused or said he wasn't Mr. Smith, Rob simply moved on to greet the next person until he eventually found Mr. Smith.

I think many people would be embarrassed if they greeted someone by the wrong name, and they may shy away from greeting strangers so robustly in the future. But not Rob. He'd happily shake a stranger's hand and call him by the wrong name. He knew that he'd eventually find Mr. Smith. He wasn't afraid of failing over and over again until he got it right.

If you get used to failing, it becomes a lot less scary, especially once you learn that failure and rejection aren't the worst things that could happen to you.

MOVE FORWARD AFTER FAILURE

If your efforts aren't successful at first, spend some time evaluating what happened and how you want to proceed. If you failed at something that isn't all that important to you, you may decide it's not worth investing more time or energy into trying again. And sometimes that makes sense. For example, I'm a terrible artist. My drawings usually consist of stick figures, but when I fail at drawing, I don't find it worth my time and energy to succeed in that one area of my life. Instead, I'd rather devote my energy to areas I feel passionate about.

If you need to overcome an obstacle in your life to help you reach your dream, however, it makes sense to try again. But doing the exact same thing over again won't help. Instead, create a plan that will increase your chance of success. Just like you need to learn from mistakes to avoid repeating them, you need to learn from failure so you can do better the next time. Sometimes that means improving your skills; at other times, that may mean looking for opportunities where your skills may be appreciated.

Elias "Walt" Disney certainly didn't become wildly successful without a few failures along the way. He originally opened a business called Laugh-O-Gram, where he contracted with the Kansas City Theater to screen his seven-minute fairy tales that combined live action with animation. Although his cartoons became popular, Walt was deeply in debt and was forced to declare bankruptcy just a few short years later.

But that didn't stop Walt. He and his brother moved to Hollywood to begin the Disney Brothers' Studio. They got a deal with a distributor who was expected to distribute a cartoon character Walt created—Oswald the Lucky Rabbit. But within a few years, the distributor stole the rights to Oswald and several of his other cartoon characters. The Disney brothers quickly produced three of their own cartoons featuring one of the characters Walt had invented—Mickey Mouse. But they failed to find distribution for it. It wasn't until sound was incorporated into film that they were able to put it into production.

Soon after, the Disney brothers' success soared. Despite the fact that it was the middle of the Great Depression, Walt began producing films that generated huge amounts of revenue. From there, he and his brother built Disneyland, a $17 million theme park. It became a huge success and they were able to use the profits to begin building Disney World. Sadly, Walt passed away before the theme park was finished.

A man who went bankrupt after a failed business venture in the cartoon industry became a multimillionaire within a few years during the Great Depression. The same cartoons that received repeated rejections from people who didn't think they would ever be a success earned him more Academy Awards than any other person in history. Even though Walt passed away almost fifty years ago, the Disney Company remains a thriving billion-dollar corporation and Walt's cartoon character, Mickey Mouse, remains the primary symbol of Disney. Clearly, Walt was a man who used his failures to motivate him to become successful.

BOUNCING BACK AFTER FAILURE WILL MAKE YOU STRONGER

Wally Amos worked as a talent agent who was known for sending his homemade chocolate chip cookies to celebrities in an effort to entice them to sign on with him. At the urging of his friends, he eventually quit working as an agent and devoted his life to baking cookies. With financial support from some of his celebrity friends, he opened his first gourmet cookie shop and called it "Famous Amos."

The store became wildly popular and the business expanded quickly. Amos opened several more stores across the country over the next decade. His success earned him national attention, including an Award of Entrepreneurial Excellence from President Ronald Reagan.

But as a high school dropout without any formal training, Amos lacked business knowledge and his million-dollar empire began to struggle. He attempted to hire people who could help, but unfortunately they also lacked the ability to turn the company around. Eventually, Amos was forced to sell his company. And not only had he experienced financial trouble with his business, but he also experienced a major financial crisis in his personal life: he lost his home to foreclosure.

A few years later he attempted to launch a new cookie company—Wally Amos Presents Chip and Cookie. But the company executives who had purchased Famous Amos sued him for using his own name. He changed the name of his new business to "Uncle Noname." His new cookie company faced steep competition and he wasn't able to make it successful. As his debt rose to over a million dollars, he was forced to file bankruptcy.

Finally, Amos opened a muffin company. But this time, he left the day-to-day operations to a partner who had expertise in food distribution. He'd learned from his previous failures that he needed help operating the business. His new business hasn't soared to the heights of his cookie business, but the company remains viable to this day.

Eventually, Amos found another break. Keebler acquired his original brand of Famous Amos cookies. And management hired him to be the product's spokesperson. Although he could have been bitter about the fact that the company he founded had achieved tremendous success now that he no longer owned it, Amos gratefully and humbly returned to urging people to buy the cookies he had begun making over thirty years ago. He's also found success as an author and a motivational speaker.

Failure can build character by challenging you in new ways. It can help you identify areas in your life that need work as well as hidden strengths you've never before recognized. In Susan's case, once she enrolled in college, she gained confidence in her ability to handle future setbacks. She no longer viewed failure as final but instead thought of it as a way to improve herself. Learning how to persevere despite failure increases your mental strength over time as you recognize how failure can improve your performance.

Understanding that you will be okay, even if you fail repeatedly, offers much peace and contentment in life. You'll no longer worry about being the best or feeling like you have to achieve the most to be appreciated. Instead, you can rest assured that with each failure, you're becoming better.

TROUBLESHOOTING AND COMMON TRAPS

Sometimes people are comfortable with failure in some areas of their lives but not others. A person may be used to failing to close the deal as a salesperson but may be very upset if she fails to become elected to city council. Identify the areas in your life where you may be more apt to give up after failure and focus on how you can learn from all the failures you experience. If you're not used to trying again after you fail, facing your fears head-on can be difficult at first. You're likely to feel a range of emotions and your thoughts may discourage you from trying again. With practice, however, you'll be able to discover how failure can be an important step in becoming successful.

WHAT'S HELPFUL

Viewing failure as a learning opportunity

Resolving to try again if your first attempt was not successful

Facing your fear of failure

Developing a new plan to increase your chance of success

Identifying and replacing irrational thoughts about failure

Focusing on improving your skills rather than showing them off

WHAT'S NOT HELPFUL

Allowing failure to stop you from reaching your goals

Considering future attempts to be a lost cause if your first attempt wasn't successful

Quitting because you don't want to tolerate discomfort

Defining a task as impossible because it didn't work the first time

Allowing yourself to think that failure is worse than it is

Refusing to participate in tasks where you are not likely to excel

CHAPTER 11

THEY DON'T FEAR ALONE TIME

All man's miseries derive from not being able to
sit quietly in a room alone.
—BLAISE PASCAL

Vanessa had asked her doctor for medication to help her sleep, but he'd recommended she try counseling first. Although she wasn't certain how counseling could help, Vanessa agreed to come and see me. She explained how she just couldn't seem to shut her mind off at night. Despite feeling exhausted, she'd often lie awake with her mind racing for several hours after she'd tried to go to sleep. Sometimes she'd second-guess certain things she'd said throughout the day while at other times, she worried about all the things she had to do tomorrow. And sometimes she had so many thoughts running through her head all at once that she didn't even know what exactly she was thinking about.

During the day, Vanessa said she didn't experience any worrisome thoughts. She worked as a real estate agent and her days were busy and often, very long. When she wasn't officially working, she could be found dining out with friends or networking with other young professionals.

The line between work and play was often blurred as she frequently received business referrals through social media or through various groups that she belonged to. She loved her active lifestyle and she enjoyed being constantly on the go. Although her job brought a lot of stress, she found her work to be quite fulfilling and she was very successful in sales.

When I asked her how often she spent any time alone or how often she ever gave herself an opportunity to just sit and think, she said, "Oh, never. I don't ever want to waste one second of my day not being productive." When I suggested to her that the reason she may be struggling to turn her mind off at night was because she didn't give her brain any time to process things during the day, she initially laughed. She said, "It's not that. I have plenty of time to think during the day. Sometimes I'm thinking about a whole bunch of things at once." I explained to her that her brain may need some downtime, a chance to unwind and I suggested she schedule some alone time in her day. Although she wasn't convinced solitude could help her sleep better, she agreed to try it as an experiment.

We discussed the various ways she could spend some time being alone with her thoughts. She agreed to try journaling for at least ten minutes a day before bed without any distractions—no TV, no cell phone, and no radio playing in the background. When she returned the following week, she said she found the silence to be a little uncomfortable, but she enjoyed journaling and thought it was helping her fall asleep a little faster.

Over the next few weeks she tried several other activities, including meditation and mindfulness exercises. To her surprise, she found a few minutes of meditation each morning to be one of the highlights of the day. And she said she felt like her mind was "quieter." She continued journaling because she felt like it gave her an outlet to sort through everything that ran through her head and the meditation taught her how to calm her racing thoughts. And although her sleeping problems weren't completely cured, she felt she was able to fall asleep much faster.

SOLITUDE PHOBIA

Spending time alone isn't at the top of most people's priority lists. For many of us, the thought of being alone just doesn't sound appealing. For others, it sounds downright scary. Do any of the points below describe you?

❒   When you have spare time, the last thing you'd likely do is just sit and think.

❒   You think spending time by yourself is boring.

❒   You like to keep the TV or a radio on for background noise when you're doing things around the house.

❒   You feel uncomfortable with silence.

❒   You equate being alone with feeling lonely.

❒   You would never enjoy doing activities, such as going to the movies or watching a concert, by yourself.

❒   You'd feel too guilty to do anything by yourself.

❒   When you have a few spare minutes in a waiting room or in between tasks, you're likely to make a phone call, send text messages, or use social media.

❒   While driving in the car by yourself, you usually keep the radio on or you talk on the phone to keep yourself entertained.

❒   Writing in a journal or meditating seems like a waste of time.

❒   You don't have time or opportunity for solitude.

Creating time to be alone with your thoughts can be a powerful experience, instrumental in helping you reach your goals. Mental strength requires you to take time out from the busyness of daily life to focus on growth.

WHY WE AVOID BEING ALONE

Vanessa didn't think solitude was a productive way to use her time. She focused so much on building a name for herself in the real estate industry that she felt guilty whenever she wasn't socializing or networking. She didn't want to miss out on an opportunity to get a new sales lead.

Although solitude has plenty of positive connotations among the major religions—Jesus, Muhammad, and Buddha were all described as appreciating solitude—being alone has developed some negative associations in modern society. Extreme cases of solitude, such as someone characterized as a "hermit," are often portrayed negatively in cartoons, fairy tales, and movies. Jokes about becoming "the old cat lady" also serve as gentle suggestions that "being alone makes you go crazy." Parents place kids in time-outs when they misbehave, which sends the message that being alone is a punishment. And the term "solitary confinement" is used to describe consequences for the worst-of-the-worst prison inmates. Although extreme solitude clearly isn't healthy, being alone seems to have received such a bad rap that even short durations of alone time can be viewed as unpleasant.

The notion that "being alone is bad" and "being surrounded by people is good" pressures us to fill our social calendars. Sometimes there's the impression that sitting home alone on a Saturday night isn't healthy or it means you're a "loser." Keeping an overbooked calendar also helps people feel important. The more your phone rings, and the more plans you make, the more important you must be.

Staying busy also serves as a wonderful distraction. If you have problems you don't want to address, why not invite your neighbors over for dinner or go shopping with some friends? After all, you won't have to think about your problems as long as you keep your brain occupied with pleasant conversation. Even if you can't spend time with other people physically, advances in technology mean that you don't ever really have to be alone. You can talk on the phone almost anywhere, use social media to be in constant contact with people, and send text messages the second you have a spare moment. You can virtually avoid being alone with your thoughts almost every minute of the day.

There are also societal pressures to be productive. People who feel like they must be accomplishing something all the time may view "alone time" as "wasting time." So they fill every spare second with activity. Whether they're cleaning the house or creating more to-do lists, they may not see much value in taking time to just sit and think because it doesn't produce immediate tangible results. In fact, they may feel guilty if they're not "getting something done."

And then, of course, some individuals just don't feel comfortable being alone. They've grown accustomed to chaos, incessant noise, and constant activity. Down time, silence, and self-care aren't words in their vocabularies. They're terrified to be alone with their thoughts because they know they may think about things that could cause them to feel uncomfortable. If they had a few spare moments, they may remember something sad or they may worry about the future. So in an attempt to keep their uncomfortable emotions at bay, they keep their minds as busy as possible.

Being alone often gets confused with being lonely. Feelings

of loneliness have been linked to poor sleep, high blood pressure, weaker immune systems, and increased stress hormones. But being alone doesn't necessarily cause loneliness. In fact, many people feel lonely when they're surrounded by others in a crowded room. Loneliness is about perceiving that no one is there for you. But solitude is about making a choice to be alone with your thoughts.

THE PROBLEM WITH FEARING SOLITUDE

The more Vanessa filled her day with constant activity, the more her brain couldn't seem to shut off at night. And the more she experienced racing thoughts, the more she tried to drown them out, which set up a perpetuating cycle. Her thoughts kept her awake at night so she began to associate "quiet time" with stress. She'd even started using the TV as background noise while she tried to fall asleep because she wanted to muffle her thoughts.

Constantly tending to our daily responsibilities and relationships can take a toll on us if we don't stop and take time to renew ourselves. Unfortunately, the benefits of solitude are often ignored or minimized. Here's what the research says are some of the major benefits that those of us who fear alone time might be missing out on:

- *Moderate alone time is good for kids.* A 1997 study called "The Emergence of Solitude as a Constructive Domain of Experience in Early Adolescence" found that fifth to ninth graders who spent moderate amounts of time alone were less likely to exhibit behavioral problems. They also scored lower on depression rating scales and had higher grade point averages.

- *Solitude at the office can increase productivity.* Although many office settings promote open work spaces and large brainstorming sessions, a 2000 study called "Cognitive Stimulation in Brainstorming" found that most people in the study performed better when they had some privacy. Spending some time away from everyone has been linked to increased productivity.

- *Alone time may increase your empathy.* When people spend time by themselves, they're more likely to show compassion for others. If you're spending a lot of time with your social circle, you're more likely to develop a "we vs. them" mentality, which can cause you to behave less compassionately toward those outside your social circle.

- *Spending time alone sparks creativity.* Many successful artists, writers, and musicians credit solitude with improving their performance, and some research suggests that spending time away from the demands of society can boost creativity.

- *Solitary skills are good for mental health.* Although there's often a lot of emphasis on the importance of social skills, evidence suggests solitary skills may be equally important for health and well-being. The ability to tolerate alone time has been linked to increased happiness, life satisfaction, and improved stress management. People who enjoy alone time also experience less depression.

- *Solitude offers restoration.* Alone time provides an opportunity to recharge your batteries. Research shows that spending time alone in nature offers rest and renewal.

Although it can be a challenge to slow down and take time out for yourself, there can be serious consequences if you don't.

My good friend Alicia experienced an extreme consequence just a few years ago. I didn't know her back then so I was surprised to hear how stress took such a cumulative effect on her life when she neglected to take care of herself.

She'd just given birth to her first child and was working twenty-five to thirty hours a week at a job that she didn't exactly love. She'd just returned to college full-time because she'd felt bad that she hadn't yet finished her degree. She also felt a lot of guilt over the fact that her hectic schedule required her to be away from her baby much of the time.

The demands of motherhood, work, and college took an emotional and physical toll on Alicia. She experienced constant anxiety, and at times, she felt like she couldn't even breathe. She began breaking out into hives and she lost her appetite. But she ignored the warning signs that her stress was reaching dangerously high levels, and she pressed onward. The day her stress finally caught up with her started out like any other day—or so she's been told. She has no recollection of it. In fact, the first thing she remembers is waking up in the hospital surrounded by her family.

She was horrified to learn that she'd been found at a gas station completely disoriented. The gas station attendant had recognized her confusion and he called for an ambulance. The ambulance crew asked her questions, like what her name was and where she lived, but she wasn't able to answer them. The only thing she could tell them was that her baby was home alone.

The police searched her car and discovered her wallet and cell phone. They contacted her family and were relieved to find out that her baby was actually safe at home being cared for by Alicia's husband. According to Alicia's family, she had seemed fine earlier in the day. She talked to her husband, got ready for school, and said her tearful good-byes to her baby. She even called her father during her commute. But somewhere along the drive to class, she became completely disoriented.

After confirming she didn't have any drugs or alcohol in her system, the doctors ruled out any possibility of stroke or head injury. When all the tests came back negative, Alicia was diagnosed with transient global amnesia—a rare form of temporary amnesia that can be triggered by severe emotional distress. Fortunately for Alicia, the symptoms cleared within a few days and she didn't suffer any long-term effects.

This incident certainly opened Alicia's eyes to the importance of taking care of herself. She says that in the past, she used to wake up thinking about all the things she "had" to get done and she spent her days rushing to get through her to-do list. Now, she slows down and takes time to enjoy each day by doing things like walking her dog and working in her yard. She's much more aware of her stress level and she takes better care of herself. Her story serves as a cautionary tale that shows the importance of slowing down and listening to our body's warning signs of stress.

GET COMFORTABLE BEING ALONE

Vanessa's days were filled with activities that easily took priority over spending time alone. The only way she could faithfully incorporate solitude into her daily routine was to schedule it and treat her alone time like all her other important appointments. She also had to view her solitary activities as practice. Learning new skills like meditation and mindfulness, and making journaling a daily habit, requires dedication. Initially, Vanessa learned about meditation by reading and watching online tutorials. But when she realized that she actually enjoyed it, she expressed an interest in taking a meditation class. She felt like the more skills she learned, the better equipped she'd be to quiet her mind at night.

PRACTICE TOLERATING SILENCE

Most of us are used to having a lot of noise surrounding us during the day. Sometimes, people actively seek out the hustle and bustle to prevent themselves from being alone with their thoughts. Do you or someone you know fall asleep with a TV or radio on for background noise? Trying to drown out your thoughts by bombarding yourself with constant noise isn't healthy. Building just a few quiet moments into your day can help recharge your batteries. Take at least ten minutes every day to sit quietly by yourself and do nothing but think. If you're used to constant noise and activity, silence may feel uncomfortable at first. However, with practice it gets easier. Use alone time to do the following:

- *Reflect on your goals.* Take a few moments every day to think about your personal or professional goals. Evaluate how you're doing and think about any changes you may want to make.

- *Pay attention to your feelings.* Check in with yourself about how you're feeling both physically and emotionally. Think about your stress level. Evaluate whether you're taking good enough care of yourself and think about any ways you could improve your life.

- *Set goals for the future.* Don't stop dreaming about what you may want the future to look like. The first step to creating the type of life you want is deciding how you want the future to look.

- *Write in a journal.* Journaling can be a powerful tool in helping you to better understand and learn from your emotions. Research studies show that writing about experiences and the emotions surrounding those experiences boosts immune systems, decreases stress, and improves mental health.

We live in a world where we can be constantly connected to people. But digital connectivity means we have fewer opportunities to be alone with our thoughts. Reaching for your phone to check for messages, scrolling through social media accounts, and reading online news stories can take up a lot of your time. Just spending a few minutes here and a few minutes there can add up to several hours a day. Constant communication interrupts your daily activities and can lead to increased stress and anxiety. Take a break from technology and incorporate some more quiet time in your daily life by trying the following:

- Turn off the TV when you're not actually watching it.

- Ride in the car without the radio playing.

- Go for a walk without taking your cell phone.

- Shut off all your electronics once in a while just to take a break.

SCHEDULE A DATE WITH YOURSELF

The key to making alone time helpful is that it has to be a choice. Elderly people who live alone and are rather isolated from society, for example, are more likely to feel lonely and less likely to benefit from solitude. But for people who live busy lives that include lots of social interaction, scheduling some alone time can provide an opportunity for rest and renewal. If you feel uncomfortable with the idea of spending time alone, the key is to create positive experiences with solitude. In addition to squeezing in a few minutes of alone time every day, schedule a date with yourself at least once a month.

By referring to it as a "date" it can remind you that you're choosing to do something on your own, not because you lack social relationships, but because it's a healthy thing to do. A 2011 research study titled "An Exercise to Teach the Psychological Benefits of Solitude: The Date with the Self" found that the vast majority of people who scheduled a date alone experienced calmness and serenity. They enjoyed the freedom to do whatever they wanted without any social constraints or expectations. The few participants who didn't find the experience enjoyable weren't yet comfortable being alone. However, increasing their exposure to alone time may help make it a more enjoyable activity for them in the future.

While fishing in a boat in the middle of a lake may offer one person a peaceful and rejuvenating experience, many other people would find the exercise to be dreadful. If you despise something, you aren't likely to keep it up long term. It's best to find some solitary activities that you enjoy so you can work them into your routine.

If you appreciate nature, consider spending time in the woods. If you love a good meal, go to a restaurant of your choice. You don't have to stay home to appreciate solitude. Instead, choose to do something that you may not normally do when you're with people. Just make sure you don't bury your nose in a book or spend the time text messaging someone. The point of a date with yourself is to be alone with your thoughts.

LEARN MEDITATION

Although once upon a time meditation was considered something that only monks or hippies did, it's starting to gain more mainstream acceptance. Many doctors, CEOs, celebrities, and politicians now appreciate the powerful impact meditation has on their mental, physical, and spiritual health. Research shows that meditation alters your brain waves, and over time, your brain physically changes. Studies have shown that regions of the brain associated with learning, memory, and emotion regulation actually begin to thicken after just a few months of meditation.

Meditation has been linked to a variety of emotional benefits, including helping those who practice to reduce negative emotions and to gain a new perspective on stressful situations. Some studies report meditation decreases anxiety and depression. Not to mention the spiritual benefit. While some claim meditation alone offers the path to enlightenment, others encourage combining prayer with meditation.

Additional research says meditation may help with a variety of physical health issues, including asthma, cancer, sleep problems, pain, and heart disease. Although some of the research has been questioned by medical experts, there's certainly no denying that meditation can have a strong influence over your body. Just ask Wim Hof.

Hof has been nicknamed the Iceman because of his ability to use meditation to tolerate extreme cold. This middle-aged Dutchman holds over twenty world records for the amazing feats he's accomplished, including being immersed in ice for well over an hour. He has climbed Mount Kilimanjaro, run marathons in the polar circle, and even hiked halfway up Mount Everest (before his trip was cut short due to a foot injury), all while wearing shorts. Skeptical researchers have performed a variety of tests on him because many believed his feats must somehow be fraudulent, but scientists concluded he's able to maintain a consistent body temperature when he meditates, despite being exposed to extreme temperatures. Hof has even begun teaching other people how to control their own thermostats through meditation.

Although being able to withstand being placed in an ice bath for an hour isn't a skill most of us need—or want for that matter—Hof's story certainly demonstrates the incredible connection between the mind and body. There are several different types of meditation so it may be helpful to conduct some research to find out which could be the best match for you. It doesn't have to be a long or formal process. Instead, meditation can just be something you do for five minutes each day to calm your mind and develop a better sense of self-awareness.

STEPS TO SIMPLE MEDITATION

In its simplest form, you can perform meditation in just a few easy steps anytime and anywhere.

- **Sit in a Relaxed Position**—Find a position that allows you to keep your spine straight, either in a chair or on the floor.

- **Focus on Your Breath**—Take deep slow breaths and really feel your breath as you inhale and as you exhale.

- **Return Your Consciousness to Your Breath**—Your mind will wander and thoughts will enter your mind. When they do, return your focus to your breathing.

MINDFULNESS SKILLS

Mindfulness is often used synonymously with meditation, but they're not exactly the same thing. Mindfulness is about developing an acute awareness of what is happening within the moment without forming judgment. In today's world we're tempted to multitask almost every minute of the day. We send text messages while walking the dog, we listen to the radio while we're cleaning the kitchen, or we try to carry on a conversation with someone while we're typing on our laptops. Instead of being mindful of what we're doing, we're zoned out. Our mind wanders in the midst of a conversation. We can't remember what we did with our car keys even though we just had them in our hands. And we can't recall whether we washed our hair already while we're in the shower.

The research on mindfulness shows a lot of similar benefits to meditation: reduced stress, fewer depressive symptoms, improved memory, decreased emotional reactivity, and even improved satisfaction in relationships. Many researchers suggest mindfulness could be the key to finding happiness. It's also been linked to improved physical health benefits such as increased immune functioning and decreased inflammation from stress.

Instead of thinking about what is "right" or "wrong" or how things "should be," mindfulness allows you to accept your thoughts for what they are in the moment. Mindfulness raises your awareness and helps you to "zone in" on each activity you're doing throughout the day. It encourages you to become more comfortable with being alone with your thoughts while also helping you to live in the moment.

Just like with meditation, you can learn mindfulness skills through books, videos, workshops, and retreats. It's taught differently by different people, so if one method of teaching doesn't work for you, explore other opportunities to learn more about mindfulness. The key to developing the skills is to remember that they take practice and dedication. But learning these skills can change the quality of your life and provide you with a new perspective on solitude.

WAYS TO PRACTICE MINDFULNESS

Many different exercises can help you begin practicing mindfulness. The more you practice, the more you'll become fully aware, and fully awake, throughout all your daily activities. Here are just a few exercises that can help you develop mindfulness:

- **Scan Your Body**—Slowly pay attention to each part of your body from the tips of your toes to the top of your head. Look for areas of your body that may be tense and practice letting go of that tension and relaxing your muscles.

- **Count to Ten**—Close your eyes and practice slowly counting to ten. Notice as your mind will likely begin to wander along the way. Refocus your attention back to slowly counting.

- **Consciously Observe**—Find an everyday object you have lying around the house, like a pen or a cup. Hold the object in your hands and focus all your attention onto it. Observe how it looks and how it feels in your hands without passing any assessments or judgments. Instead, try to focus on the here and now.

- **Eat a Mindful Bite of Food**—Take a small piece of food, such as a raisin or a nut, and explore it with as many senses as possible. Look at it and notice the texture and color. Next, observe how it feels in your hand. Then, pay attention to how it smells. Now put it in your mouth and taste it. Chew slowly and pay attention to the flavor and how it feels in your mouth for at least twenty seconds.

HOW EMBRACING ALONE TIME WILL MAKE YOU STRONGER

Once Vanessa learned the tools necessary to help reduce her racing thoughts, she no longer thought she needed medication to help her sleep. Instead, she could use meditation and mindfulness to quiet her mind before she went to sleep. She also noticed how her skills made a difference in her professional life. Throughout the day, her focus was better. She felt like she was able to be more productive and she no longer felt as disorganized, despite her chaotic schedule.

Learning skills to quiet your mind and be alone with your thoughts can be a powerful and life-changing experience. In his book *10% Happier,* Dan Harris describes how meditation changed his life. As the coanchor of ABC's *Nightline* and a weekend anchor for *Good Morning America,* he needed to present his best self live on the air every day. But one day he suffered a panic attack in the middle of reading a news report. As he became overwhelmed with sudden anxiety, he struggled to speak and grew short of breath, forcing him to cut the segment short. He later learned that his panic attack—which he refers to as the most embarrassing moment of his life—likely resulted from his attempts to self-medicate his recent depression with ecstasy and cocaine. Even though he hadn't gotten high for weeks, the effects had lingered in his brain. The panic attack motivated him to quit self-medicating and he began a new quest to find out how to manage his stress.

Around the same time, Harris was assigned to report on a series about religion. As part of the assignment, he was introduced to meditation. Although he initially felt that meditation wouldn't be anything he'd ever be interested in, the more he learned, the more open-minded he became. Eventually, he discovered first-hand how meditation could provide him with realistic strategies to calm the anxious thoughts in his head.

Although he acknowledges he was initially uncomfortable with telling people he'd started meditating, he recognizes how much sharing his story could help other people. He's clear that meditation didn't magically fix everything in his life, but he says it improved his mood by 10 percent. In his book he says, "Until we look directly at our minds we don't really know what our lives are about."

Spending time alone, whether you choose to meditate or you use some quiet time to simply reflect on your goals, is the best way to really get to know yourself. Just like it's important to spend quality time with loved ones that you want to get to know, it's imperative that you spend time getting to know yourself. Developing an improved sense of self-awareness can help you continue to recognize what's holding you back from reaching your full potential.

TROUBLESHOOTING AND COMMON TRAPS

If you ever find yourself dreaming of being stranded on a desert island, it means you're well overdue for some solitude. Don't be afraid of scheduling time alone. It's not selfish or a waste of time. Instead, it could be one of the most beneficial things you could ever do. It can improve your life in a multitude of ways and can help you learn how to enjoy every moment, instead of rushing from one task to the next without being tuned in to what's really going on around you.

WHAT'S HELPFUL

Learning how to appreciate silence

Taking a few minutes every day to be alone with your thoughts

Scheduling a date with yourself at least one time a month

Learning how to meditate to quiet your mind

Practicing mindfulness skills to focus on one task at a time

Journaling to sort out your emotions

Reflecting on your progress and goals daily

WHAT'S NOT HELPFUL

Keeping background noise on at all times

Hurrying from one activity to the next and focusing on constantly producing something

Filling your calendar with social engagements without leaving any time for yourself

Believing that meditation couldn't possibly be helpful

Multitasking and zoning out throughout the day

Assuming that journaling is a waste of time

Looking at your to-do list and judging each day's progress by how many things you've accomplished

CHAPTER 12

THEY DON'T FEEL THE WORLD OWES THEM ANYTHING

Don't go around saying the world owes you a living. The world owes you nothing. It was here first.
—ROBERT JONES BURDETTE

Lucas entered therapy because people in his company's Human Resources Department suggested that he take advantage of their employee assistance program to address some problems he'd recently had at work. Through the program, Lucas could receive a handful of counseling sessions completely free of charge.

Lucas had recently been hired at his first big job since getting his MBA. He was excited about the position and he really believed in the company he worked for. But he didn't feel like his coworkers were as thrilled to have him on board. He explained how he often made suggestions about how his supervisor could increase the company's profitability, and he tried to help his coworkers become more efficient and productive. He offered ideas at the weekly team meetings, but he didn't think anyone was listening to him. He'd even scheduled a meeting with his boss asking to be promoted to a leadership position. He thought having more authority would make other people more willing to take his advice.

Much to his dismay, his supervisor wasn't interested in promoting him. Instead, the supervisor told Lucas to "tone it down" if he wanted to remain employed, because his fellow coworkers were already complaining about his attitude. Following the meeting, Lucas had gone to his company's Human Resources office to complain and it was then that they recommended he receive some counseling.

As Lucas and I talked, he said he felt like he deserved a promotion. Even though he was new to the company, he was certain he had great ideas about how to make the business more profitable and he figured he should be paid more than his current salary. We explored his assumption that he was an extremely valuable employee and how his employer might see things differently. We also discussed the consequences of making such a bold assumption. He recognized that his inference was clearly causing some problems for him at the office—his coworkers, and most likely his supervisor, were annoyed.

Once Lucas was able to see how his "know-it-all" attitude was rubbing people the wrong way, we discussed what it was probably like for his coworkers to work with him. Some of them had been with the company for decades and were slowly trying to work their way up the corporate ladder. Lucas said he understood how some of them might feel frustrated when someone who was fresh out of college started offering them advice. He admitted that he often thought of them as "stupid," and we discussed how these types of thoughts would only fuel his desire to behave in a bossy manner. He participated in trying to reframe those thoughts so that he could recognize the value that long-term employees offered the company. Instead of viewing coworkers as "stupid" he reacted by telling himself that they simply did things differently. When he began thinking he was a better employee than someone else, he reminded himself he was fresh out of college and still had a lot to learn.

Lucas agreed to create a list of behaviors that his employer would want to see from the company's best employees. When he was done with that list, we reviewed how many of those behaviors he exhibited. He acknowledged that he didn't do all of the things on the list—like support other employees and show respectful behavior. Instead, he was too focused on showing off and making demands.

Lucas agreed to take his newfound insight and apply it to his behavior at the office. When he returned for his next appointment a couple of weeks later, he shared some of the changes he'd been working on. He said he had stopped offering so much unsolicited advice to others. He found that when he pulled back and stopped trying to force people to listen to him, they were more inclined to ask him questions and seek out his opinion. He thought this was definitely a step in the right direction and he felt confident he could continue to work on being a valuable employee rather than the invaluable resource he had previously assumed he was.

CENTER OF THE UNIVERSE

We're all inclined to want our fair share in life. However, the belief that you're owed something simply because of who you are or what you've been through isn't healthy. Do you respond positively to any of the points below?

- ❏ You think you perform better than average at most tasks, like driving or interacting with other people.

- ❏ You're more likely to talk your way out of problems rather than accept the consequences.

- ❏ You believe you were born to be successful.

- ❏ You think your self-worth is tied to your material wealth.

- ❏ You believe you deserve to be happy.

- ❏ You think you've dealt with your share of problems in life and it's your turn to have good things happen to you.

❐ You enjoy talking about yourself more than hearing about other people.

❐ You think you're smart enough to succeed without having to work hard.

❐ You sometimes buy things you can't afford but justify it by telling yourself that you're worth it.

❐ You consider yourself an expert in many things.

Believing that you shouldn't have to work as hard or shouldn't have to go through the same process as everyone else because you're the exception to the rule isn't healthy. But you can learn how to stop complaining about not getting what you deserve and start focusing on how to become mentally strong enough that you'll no longer feel entitled.

WHY WE FEEL THE WORLD OWES US SOMETHING

Lucas had grown up as an only child and throughout his life, his parents had assured him he was a natural-born leader who was meant to be successful. So when he graduated from college, he felt confident he was destined for greatness. He presumed that any employer would immediately recognize his talent and feel fortunate to have him on their team.

Whether it's someone who has dealt with unfortunate circumstances and thinks he deserves something to make up for it, or it's someone who thinks she's better than everyone else and deserves to be rewarded for it, people like Lucas are everywhere. And while we're good at noticing this trait in other people, the fact is, all of us feel entitled at one time or another and we often lack the insight to recognize it in ourselves.

We live in a world where rights and privileges frequently get confused. Often, people think they have a "right to be happy" or a "right to be treated respectfully," even if it means they have to infringe on others' rights to get what they want. Instead of trying to earn privileges, they behave as if society is somehow indebted to them. Advertising tempts us to buy products by promoting self-indulgence and materialism. The idea that "You deserve it," whether you can afford it or not, leads many among us to go deeply into debt.

A feeling that the world owes you something isn't always about a sense of superiority. Sometimes it is about a sense of injustice. A person who had a difficult childhood, for example, may max out his credit cards as he buys himself all the things he never had as a kid. He may think the world owes him the opportunity to have nice things, since he missed out on a lot as a youngster. This type of entitlement can be just as detrimental as when people think they're superior.

Jean Twenge, a psychologist and author of *Generation Me* and *The Narcissism Epidemic,* has conducted many studies on narcissism and entitlement. Her studies have found that younger generations have an increased desire for material wealth and a decreased desire to work. She suggests several possible reasons for this disconnect including:

- *The focus on helping kids develop self-esteem has gone overboard.* School programs aimed at improving self-esteem teach kids that they're all special. Allowing children to wear shirts that say things like IT'S ALL ABOUT ME or telling them repeatedly, "You're the best," fuels their inflated beliefs about self-importance.

- *Overindulgent parenting prevents children from learning how to accept responsibility for their behavior.* When kids are given whatever they want and they don't have to experience consequences for misbehavior, they don't learn the value of earning things. Instead, they're given an overabundance of material possessions and accolades regardless of their behavior.

- *Social media fuels mistaken beliefs about self-importance.* Young people can't imagine a world without "selfies" and self-promotional blogs. It's unclear if social media actually fuels narcissism or it simply serves as an outlet for people to announce their underlying beliefs of superiority. But there is evidence that suggests people turn to social media to boost their self-esteem.

THE PROBLEM WITH A SENSE OF ENTITLEMENT

Lucas's sense of entitlement certainly wasn't winning him any friends at the office. It also wasn't likely to help him gain a promotion any time soon.

An entitlement mentality prevents you from earning things based on merit. You'll be less likely to work hard when you're busy complaining that you're not getting what you're owed. Instead, you'll expect that you should have things based on who you are or what you've been through. You won't be able to accept responsibility for your behavior when you're focused on trying to stake your claim over what you think the world owes you.

You'll also make unrealistic demands of people or be too focused on gaining what you think you deserve to be able to contribute to a relationship in a meaningful way.

If you are always demanding, "I deserve to be cared for and treated well," you may have trouble offering the type of love and respect that will attract a partner who treats you kindly.

When you're focused on yourself, it is extremely challenging to be empathetic. Why donate time and money to other people if you're always thinking things like *I deserve to buy nice things for myself*? Instead of experiencing the joy of giving, you'll be too fixated on what you're not getting.

When you don't get everything you want entitlement can lead to feelings of bitterness as you'll think you were somehow victimized. Instead of enjoying all that you have and all that you're free to do, you'll focus on all that you don't have and all the things you can't do. You'll likely miss out on some of the best things in life.

GET OVER YOURSELF

Lucas needed to understand how his sense of entitlement affected him and those around him. Once his eyes were opened to the way that other people perceived him, he was able to begin changing the way he thought about his coworkers as well as the way he behaved toward them. A willingness to work hard, combined with some humility, helped Lucas remain employed.

DEVELOP SELF-AWARENESS OF YOUR SENSE OF ENTITLEMENT

We see it all the time in the media—wealthy people, celebrities, and politicians acting like the normal laws and rules don't apply to them because they're special. Or take, for instance, the teenage boy who was placed on trial for murder after killing four people in a drunken driving accident in Texas. The defense team suggested the boy was suffering from "affluenza"—meaning he thought he was above the law. The argument was that the teenager shouldn't be held responsible because he grew up in a wealthy family with parents who had coddled him and never required him to accept any responsibility for his behavior. The teen was ultimately sentenced to a substance abuse rehabilitation program and probation, and he didn't receive any jail time. It's these types of stories that make us question whether we as a society are becoming more tolerant of the idea that the world does owe certain people more than others.

More subtle versions of entitlement have also become commonplace. If you don't land that dream job, the common reaction from friends is usually something along the lines of "Well, something better will come your way" or "You deserve something good to happen to you after all this." But even though these statements are made with the best of intentions, the world doesn't really work like that. No matter whether you're the smartest person on the planet or you've persevered through life's roughest circumstances, you don't become more deserving of good fortune than anyone else.

Try to become more aware of these subtle moments of entitlement. Look for thoughts that indicate you have some underlying beliefs about what the world owes you, such as:

- *I deserve better than this.*

- *I'm not following that law because it's stupid.*

- *I'm more valuable than this.*

- *I was meant to be highly successful.*

- *Good things will come my way.*

- *There's always been something really special about me.*

Most people who feel a sense of entitlement lack self-awareness. They think everyone else perceives them the same way they perceive themselves. Pay attention to the thoughts that you have and keep these truths in mind:

- *Life isn't meant to be fair.* There isn't a higher power or any person on Earth who ensures that all humans are dealt a fair or equal hand. Some people have more positive experiences than others. That's life but it doesn't mean you're owed anything if you were dealt a bad hand.

- *Your problems aren't unique.* Although no one else's life is exactly like yours, other people experience the same types of problems, sorrows, and tragedies as you. There are likely many people on the planet who have overcome worse. No one promised life would be easy.

- *You have choices in how you respond to disappointments.* Even if you can't change the situation, you can choose how to respond. You can decide to deal with problems, circumstances, or tragedies that come your way without developing a victim mentality.

- *You aren't more deserving.* Although you're different from everyone else, there's nothing about you that makes you better than other people. There's no reason that you should inherently have good things happen to you or that you shouldn't have to put in time and effort to reap the benefits.

FOCUS ON GIVING, NOT TAKING

I first heard about "Sarah's House" from a radio commercial that was advertising an upcoming fund-raising event. It wasn't until later that I learned that Sarah and I had actually grown up in the same town. In fact, I'd seen her before. The last night of my mom's life, we were at a basketball game and I recall a set of twins playing on the team. One of them was Sarah Robinson.

I've since met Sarah's twin sister, Lindsay Turner, and she's told me all about Sarah. When Sarah was twenty-four, she was diagnosed with a brain tumor. She underwent surgery and chemotherapy for a year and a half before losing her battle to cancer. Throughout the course of her treatment, Sarah didn't focus on how unfair it was that she got cancer. Instead, she was too busy focusing on her mission to help other people.

Sarah met other cancer patients at her treatment center, and she was horrified to learn that many of them had to drive a great distance to get treatment. Living in rural Maine meant some patients were making a five-hour round-trip drive five days a week for six weeks at a time because they couldn't afford hotel rooms. Some of them were even sleeping in their vehicles at the Walmart parking lot. She knew this wasn't a good way for anyone to fight a battle for their life.

Sarah wanted to help and initially joked that she could buy bunk beds and let everyone sleep at her house, but she knew that wouldn't be a long-term solution. So she came up with the idea to create a hospitality house close to the treatment center. Sarah had already been a member of her local Rotary Club for several years. The club's motto is "service above self," which is clearly something Sarah believed in. She pitched the idea to the club and its members agreed to help her create a hospitality house.

She became passionate about turning this idea into a reality and she worked tirelessly to get it off the ground. In fact, her family says that even while she was undergoing chemotherapy, she'd often get up in the night to work on this project. Even as Sarah's health deteriorated her attitude remained positive. She told her family, "I'm not leaving the party early, I'm getting there first." Not only did her faith in God remain strong, but so did her desire to make the hospitality house a reality.

Sarah passed away in December of 2011, at the age of twenty-six. And just like she'd asked them to do, her family and friends are working to make "Sarah's House" a reality. Within eighteen months, they raised almost a million dollars. Even Sarah's daughter has become involved in the fund-raising. She keeps a jar with the words *Sarah's House* written on it, and she donates the money she earns from selling lemonade for "Momma." Without a single paid employee, volunteers have worked tirelessly to turn a former furniture store into a nine-room hospitality house that won't ever turn patients away.

Although most people diagnosed with a terminal illness may ask "Why me?," that wasn't Sarah's mentality. As her health deteriorated to the point that she could no longer put on her own pajamas, and her husband had to dress her, she wrote in her journal, "I'm the luckiest woman alive!!!"

"I have a very firm affirmation that I have 'left it all on the field' (the field of life that is)," she wrote in another journal entry. "I have not held back, I do not regret, the people in my life know what they mean to me and I will always openly project that." Sarah certainly did give life everything she had and it's probably one of the reasons she was able to face death with such courage, even at such a young age. Shortly before she died, she revealed that one of her wishes was to inspire others to join their local civic organizations because, "that's what life is all about." She made it clear that when people are dying, no one ever wishes that they had spent another day at the office. Instead, they wish they had spent more time helping others.

Sarah never wasted a minute feeling like the world owed her anything because she had cancer. Instead, she focused on what she could give to the world. She helped others without expecting to be owed anything in return.

BEHAVE LIKE A TEAM PLAYER

Whether you're trying to get along with your coworkers, create genuine friendships, or improve a romantic relationship, you won't be able to do so unless you're a team player. Stop focusing on what you think would make things fair and instead try the following:

- *Focus on your efforts, not your importance.* Instead of paying attention to how overqualified you may think you are, focus on your efforts. There is always room for improvement.

- *Accept criticism gracefully.* If someone offers you feedback, don't be quick to say, "Well, that person is stupid." Their feedback is based on how they perceive you, which of course is likely to be different from how you perceive yourself. Be willing to evaluate criticism and consider whether you want to change your behavior.

- *Acknowledge your flaws and weaknesses.* Everyone has flaws and weaknesses, whether we like to admit them or not. Recognizing that you have insecurities, problems, and unattractive characteristics about yourself can ensure you don't develop an inflated self-perception. Just don't use those weaknesses as an excuse about why the world owes you more.

- *Stop and think about how other people feel.* Rather than focusing on what you think you deserve in life, take time to think about how other people may feel. Increasing empathy for others can decrease your inflated sense of self-importance.

- *Don't keep score.* Whether you were able to successfully give up a drug addiction or you helped an elderly person across the street, the world doesn't owe you anything in return. Don't keep score of your good deeds—or the reasons you've felt wronged—because you'll only set yourself up for disappointment when you don't ever receive what you think you're owed.

PRACTICING HUMILITY MAKES YOU STRONGER

In 1940, Wilma Rudolph was born prematurely. Weighing only four pounds, she was a sickly child. At the age of four, she contracted polio. Her left leg and foot became twisted as a result and she had to wear a leg brace until she was nine. She then had to wear an orthopedic shoe for an additional two years. With the help of physical therapy, Rudolph was finally able to walk normally by the age of twelve and for the first time in her life, she could join her school's sports teams.

It was then that she discovered her love and talent for running and she began training. By the time she was sixteen, she earned a spot on the 1956 Olympic team and as the youngest member on the team, she won the bronze medal in the 4 x 100 relay. When Rudolph returned home, she began training for the next Olympics. She enrolled at Tennessee State University and kept on running. In the 1960 Olympics, Rudolph became the first American woman to win three gold medals in a single Olympics Game. She was hailed as "the fastest woman in history." Rudolph retired from competition at the age of twenty-two.

Although many people blame their problems in adulthood on difficulties they encountered during childhood, Rudolph certainly didn't. She could have attributed any shortcomings she experienced to the fact that she had been so sick as a child, or that as an African American woman she faced racism, or that she grew up in poverty in an inner city. But Rudolph didn't think the world owed her anything. Rudolph once said, "It doesn't matter what you're trying to accomplish. It's all a matter of discipline. I was determined to discover what life held for me beyond the inner-city streets." That's how she went from walking with a leg brace to winning an Olympic medal within five years. Although Rudolph passed away in 1994, her legacy lives on and she continues to inspire new generations of athletes.

Insisting that you're entitled to more than you have isn't likely to help you in life. It will only waste your time and energy and lead to disappointment. Lucas discovered that when he stopped trying to show off, and he became open to learning, he was able to improve his job performance. And ultimately, that was necessary to help him work toward his goal of advancing in the company.

When you stop demanding that you need more and are able to be satisfied with what you have, you'll reap tremendous benefits in life. You'll move forward with a sense of peace and contentment without experiencing bitterness and selfishness.

TROUBLESHOOTING AND COMMON TRAPS

Increasing your mental strength sometimes requires you to accept what the world gives you without complaining that you deserve better. And although it's tempting to say we don't ever feel like the world owes us anything—after all, it's not a very attractive quality—there are times that we all think we're owed more in some fashion. Pay close attention to the times and areas in your life where this attitude likely sneaks in, and take steps to rid yourself of this self-destructive mentality.

WHAT'S HELPFUL

Developing healthy amounts of self-esteem

Recognizing areas of your life where you believe you are superior

Focusing on what you have to give, rather than what you want to take

Giving back to other people in need

Behaving like a team player

Thinking about other people's feelings

WHAT'S NOT HELPFUL

Becoming overconfident in yourself and your abilities

Insisting you are better than most people at almost everything

Keeping score about all the things you think you deserve in life

Refusing to give to others because you think you don't have what you deserve

Looking out for what's best for you all the time

Only taking your own feelings into consideration

CHAPTER 13

THEY DON'T EXPECT IMMEDIATE RESULTS

Patience, persistence and perspiration make an unbeatable combination for success.
—NAPOLEON HILL

Marcy couldn't identify any specific reason why she was unhappy in her life, but she described an overall sense of dissatisfaction. She explained her marriage was "okay" and she had a fairly healthy relationship with her two children. She didn't really mind her job, but it certainly wasn't her dream career. She just didn't feel as happy as she'd like to be and she thought she might be more stressed than the average person, but she couldn't offer any specifics.

She'd spent years reading self-help book after self-help book but none of them were life altering. And the three sessions of therapy she'd tried a couple of years ago hadn't really changed her life either. She was pretty certain that more therapy wouldn't help, but she thought if she could show her doctor that she'd tried it for a few sessions, he might be willing to prescribe medication that would make her feel happier. She was up front in saying that she didn't really have any time or energy to devote to therapy at this point in her life.

I acknowledged to Marcy that she was right—if she didn't want to put in any effort, therapy wouldn't do any good. But I also explained that medication usually wasn't a quick fix either. In fact, most antidepressants take at least four to six weeks before people notice any type of change. Sometimes it takes many months to find the right medication and the right dosage. And some people never experience any type of relief at all.

I clarified that therapy didn't need to be a lifelong commitment. Instead, short-term therapy could be effective. It wasn't the amount of sessions that made the difference—it was the amount of work she did that would determine how successful therapy would be and how quickly she'd see results. Armed with that new knowledge, Marcy said she'd need to spend some time thinking about her options. Within a few days, she called back and said she wanted to give therapy a try and she was willing to make it a priority in her life.

Within the first few sessions, it became clear that Marcy expected immediate results in many areas of her life. Whenever she tried anything new, whether it was an exercise class or a hobby, she gave up quickly if she wasn't seeing the results she wanted. She sometimes tried to improve her marriage because she really wanted a "wonderful" relationship, and not just a so-so one. For a few weeks, she'd work on being the best wife she could be, but when she didn't experience marital bliss right away, she'd give up.

Over the next few weeks we discussed how her expectations of immediate gratification had affected her not just personally but also professionally. She had always wanted to get her master's degree so she could advance in her career, but she felt like it would take forever so she didn't bother. Now that she'd put off her two-year degree for another ten years, she felt more frustrated about it than ever.

Marcy kept attending therapy and over the next few months, she discovered strategies to help her tolerate frustration and learn patience. She began looking at several goals she wanted to reach—including furthering her education and improving her marriage. As she identified small, action steps she could take, we discussed how she could measure her progress. Marcy tackled her new goals with a new attitude—she knew it would take time to see major results and she prepared herself for that. She noticed that her newfound resolve to create change helped improve her life as she gained new hope for the future and her ability to move forward one step at a time.

PATIENCE ISN'T YOUR VIRTUE

Although we live in a fast-paced world, we can't get everything we want instantly. Whether you're hoping to improve your marriage or you want to start your own business, expecting immediate results can set you up to fail. Do any of the points below sound familiar?

❐ You don't believe good things come to those who wait.

❐ You think of time as money and you don't want to risk wasting a single second.

❐ Patience isn't your strong suit.

❐ If you don't see immediate results, you're likely to presume what you're doing isn't working.

❐ You want things done now.

❐ You often look for shortcuts so you don't have to expend as much effort and energy getting what you want.

❐ You feel frustrated when other people don't seem to go at your pace.

❐ You give up when you aren't seeing results fast enough.

❐ You have trouble sticking to your goals.

❐ You think everything should happen fast.

❐ You tend to underestimate how long it will take to reach your goals or accomplish something.

Mentally strong people recognize that a quick fix isn't always the best solution. A willingness to develop realistic expectations and an understanding that success doesn't happen overnight is necessary if you want to reach your full potential.

WHY WE EXPECT IMMEDIATE RESULTS

Marcy felt like she'd just gotten impatient as she grew older. When things didn't happen at her pace, she became demanding. In fact, her mantra had become "I'm not getting any younger." Her aggressive demeanor worked well in a few areas of her life—her children and her coworkers were more likely to comply when they knew she meant business. But that impatience spilled over into other areas of her life where it didn't serve her so well and it damaged some of her relationships.

Marcy isn't alone in her quest for immediate relief from distress. One in ten Americans takes an antidepressant. Although antidepressants can help people with clinical depression, research shows the vast majority of people taking them haven't ever been diagnosed with depression by a mental health professional. Still, plenty of people want to take medication as a shortcut to improving their lives. The same goes for children. Parents who have kids with behavior problems often ask for a "pill" to manage them. Although legitimate attention-deficit hyperactivity disorder can respond to medication, there isn't a pill that magically makes kids behave.

We live in a fast-moving world of "no lines, no waiting." We no longer have to send a letter and wait several days for it to arrive. Instead, we can use e-mail to transmit information anywhere in the world within seconds. We don't have to wait for commercials to end before resuming our favorite TV shows. On-demand movies mean we can watch almost any movie we want in an instant. Microwaves and fast food mean we can get our food in a matter of minutes. And we can order almost anything we want online and have it delivered to our doors within twenty-four hours.

Not only does our fast-paced world discourage us from waiting, but there are always stories floating around about someone who has become an "overnight success." You hear about a musician who gets discovered from a YouTube video or a reality star who becomes an instant celebrity. Or start-ups that make millions of dollars as soon as they get off the ground. These types of accounts fuel our desire to get immediate results from whatever we're doing.

Despite the stories about people and businesses achieving immediate results, in reality, success is rarely instant. Twitter's founder spent eight years creating mobile and social products before founding Twitter. Apple's first iPod took three years and four versions before sales really took off. Amazon wasn't profitable for the first seven years. There is often folklore about these businesses that suggests they became overnight successes, but that's because people are looking at the end result and not at all the work it took to get there.

So it's no wonder we have come to expect immediate results in other areas of our lives. Whether we're trying to rid ourselves of bad habits, like overeating or drinking too much, or we're working toward goals like paying off debt or earning a college degree, we want it now. Here are some more reasons why we expect immediate results:

- *We lack patience.* It's evident in our everyday behavior that we expect things to happen immediately. If we don't get results, we give up. A study conducted by Ramesh Sitaraman, a computer science professor at UMass Amherst, found that when it comes to technology, our patience lasts two seconds. If within two seconds, an online video doesn't load, people start leaving the website. Clearly, our patience is short and when we don't get the results we want right away, it affects our behavior.

- *We overestimate our abilities.* Sometimes we tend to think that we'll do so well at something that we'll see results right away. Someone may incorrectly assume he's likely to become the best performing salesperson at his company within his first month of employment or someone else may assume he can lose twenty pounds in just two weeks. Overestimating your abilities can leave you feeling disappointed when you find that you're not able to perform as well as you'd predicted.

- *We underestimate how long change takes.* We're so used to technology accomplishing things quickly, we incorrectly assume that change in all the areas of our lives can happen fast. We lose sight of the fact that personal change, business operations, and people don't move nearly as fast as technology.

THE PROBLEM WITH EXPECTING IMMEDIATE RESULTS

Marcy was missing out on new opportunities because she only wanted to do the things in life that would be quick and painless. Although she devoted countless hours to reading self-help books, she didn't apply any of the information to her life. She'd always given up on therapy quickly and wanted to find a pill to magically change her life. She overlooked many chances to improve her life because she always expected immediate results.

Unrealistic expectations about how easy it is to make changes and get fast results can set you up to fail. In a 1997 research study titled "End-of-Treatment Self-Efficacy: A Predicator of Abstinence," researchers reported they found that patients who were overly confident about their ability to abstain from alcohol when they're discharged from a rehabilitation facility were more likely to relapse compared to patients who were less confident. Overconfidence may cause you to assume that you'll reach your goal with ease, and then if you don't get immediate results, you may struggle to stay on course.

Expecting immediate results can also cause you to prematurely abandon your efforts. If you aren't seeing results right away, you may incorrectly assume your efforts aren't working. A business owner who invests money in a new marketing campaign may assume her efforts didn't work because she doesn't see an instant increase in sales. But perhaps her investment in advertising is increasing brand recognition that will lead to a steady increase in sales over the long term. Or maybe someone who goes to the gym for a month doesn't see bigger muscles when he looks in the mirror, so he assumes his workouts aren't effective. But, in reality, he's slowly making progress that will take many months, not just weeks. And there's research that suggests we're giving up on our goals faster than ever before. A 1972 study called "Self-Initiated Attempts to Change Behavior: A Study of New Year's Resolutions" found that 25 percent of the study's participants abandoned their New Year's resolutions after fifteen weeks. Fast-forward to 1989, and 25 percent of people were abandoning their resolutions after only one week.

Here are some other potential negative consequences that can occur when you expect to see immediate results:

- *You may be tempted to take shortcuts.* If you're not getting fast enough results, you may fall prey to hurrying things along in an unnatural manner. If a dieter isn't getting the results she wants in a couple of weeks, she may go on a crash diet in an attempt to speed up the process. Athletes who want to get stronger and faster may take performance-enhancing drugs. Shortcuts can have dangerous consequences.

- *You won't be prepared for the future.* Wanting everything now will prevent you from looking at the long-term picture. The desire to get immediate results is evident in the way people view investments. People want to see a return on their investment now, not thirty years from now. The 2014 Retirement Confidence Survey found that 36 percent of Americans have less than $1,000 in savings or investments. Clearly, there are likely to be economic factors involved that prevent people from placing money into retirement, but our desire for instant gratification is also likely to play a role. People don't want to set aside money in long-term investments because they want to enjoy their money today.

- *Unrealistic expectations can cause you to draw the wrong conclusions.* If you expect immediate results, you may be tempted to assume you've seen enough to develop a conclusion, but in reality, you may not have given it enough time to get an accurate picture. A person who is unable to get a business off the ground in a year may decide he's a complete failure in the business world because he didn't make any money. But in reality, he just didn't give his start-up enough time to turn it into a viable business venture.

- *It leads to negative and uncomfortable emotions.* When your expectations aren't met, you're likely to become disappointed, impatient, and frustrated. When you experience increased negative emotions, your progress may be slowed and you may be tempted to give up altogether when you think you should be seeing a better outcome.

- *You may engage in behavior that sabotages your goals.* Unrealistic expectations may influence your behavior and make it more difficult to achieve the results you want. If you expect a cake to be baked quickly, you may open the oven door to check it repeatedly. Each time you open the oven, you allow heat to escape, which ultimately means the cake will take even longer to bake. When you expect things to happen fast, your behavior may interfere with your efforts before you even realize it.

COMMIT TO THE LONG HAUL

Once Marcy accepted that she wouldn't see immediate results, she had to decide whether to commit to making changes in therapy. She was tired enough of other things not working that she agreed to try therapy, and she knew that a partial commitment wasn't going to help. By the end of treatment, she also recognized that self-improvement—like other changes in life—doesn't happen immediately and she'd need to continue to devote time and energy to personal growth over the course of her life.

CREATE REALISTIC EXPECTATIONS

You won't pay off $100,000 in debt on a $50,000 income in six months. You can't lose twenty-five pounds in time for swimsuit season if you wait until May to begin exercising. And you probably won't climb the corporate ladder during your first year at the office. But if you have these types of expectations, you may never reach your goals. Create realistic expectations that will keep you energized over the long haul. Here are some strategies to create realistic expectations about any goal:

- *Don't underestimate how difficult change is.* Accept that doing something different, striving to reach a goal, or giving up a bad habit will be hard.

- *Avoid placing a definite time limit on reaching your goal.* It's helpful to create an estimated time limit on when you should see results, but avoid creating a definitive timeline. For example, some people claim you can establish a good habit or break a bad habit in a certain number of days (the magic numbers seem to be either twenty-one or thirty-eight days depending on which study you read). But if you step back and think about that, clearly that's not reality. It would only take me about two days to get used to eating ice cream for dessert every day and about six months to get out of the habit of having a cup of coffee with my breakfast. So don't assign a timeline based on what you think "should be." Instead, be flexible and understand that a lot of factors will influence when you will see results.

- *Don't overestimate how much better the results will make your life.* Sometimes people think, *If I lose twenty pounds, every aspect of my life will be much better.* But when they begin losing weight, they don't see the miraculous results they had imagined. They experience disappointment because they overestimated and exaggerated the outcome.

RECOGNIZE THAT PROGRESS ISN'T ALWAYS OBVIOUS

Several other therapists and I used to facilitate a parenting group. The parents who attended mostly had preschool-age children, and the most common behavior problem they wanted addressed was temper tantrums. Of course, young children are notorious for their abilities to throw themselves down on the ground, scream, and kick when they're not getting what they want. So as part of the program, parents were encouraged to ignore attention-seeking behaviors. Despite warnings that behaviors would sometimes get worse before they got better, parents frequently became convinced that ignoring just didn't work. When asked how they knew it wasn't working, they'd say things like, "He just started screaming louder" or "She got up and ran over to me and threw herself back on the ground to continue her tantrum right in front of me!"

What these parents hadn't yet realized was that their attempts at ignoring were working. The kids were getting the message that their parents weren't going to give in to them anymore, and these savvy little four-year-olds were upping their game. They figured if Mom or Dad wasn't giving in when they screamed a little, they'd better scream louder to get what they wanted. And each time parents gave in, it reinforced the kids' temper tantrums. But if parents could ignore attention-seeking behaviors consistently, their kids would learn that temper tantrums weren't an effective way to get what they wanted. Parents often needed reassurance that just because their child's behavior seemed to be getting worse, it didn't mean their parenting strategies weren't effective.

Progress toward your goal might not always be in a straight line. Sometimes things have to get worse before they can get better. And other times, you might feel like you take two steps forward and one step back. If you can remember to look at your long-term goals, however, it will help you put setbacks into perspective. Before you set out to reach your goal—whether you want to start a new business or you want to learn meditation—consider how you'll measure progress by asking yourself the following questions:

- *How will I know if what I'm doing is working?*

- *What is a realistic time frame to see initial results?*

- *What kind of results can I realistically expect to see within one week, one month, six months, and one year?*

- *How will I know that I'm staying on track toward my goal?*

PRACTICE DELAYING GRATIFICATION

Delayed gratification is something that some people seem to be better at than others. But the truth is, everyone can fall prey to the lure of instant gratification. Immediate gratification is at the heart of many problems, including some major physical and mental health issues, financial problems, and addictions. While one person might not be able to resist a cookie that isn't on his diet, someone else might not be able to put down the alcohol that causes so many problems in her life. Even people who are good at delaying gratification in some areas of their lives are likely to have weaknesses in others.

Take, for example, the case of Daniel "Rudy" Ruettiger, whose inspirational story was turned into a movie in the early 1990s. His was the ultimate story of an underdog who persevered through hard work and dedication. As the third child of fourteen children, Rudy had dreamed of someday going to Notre Dame. But he struggled with dyslexia and had a difficult time academically. He applied to Notre Dame but was rejected three times. So he enrolled in nearby Holy Cross College. After two years of hard work, he was finally accepted to Notre Dame in 1974.

Not only did he aspire to be a successful student, but he also dreamed of playing on the football team. But at only five foot six and 165 pounds, he didn't look like a contender. Notre Dame, however, allowed members of the student body to become walk-on candidates. So Rudy earned a spot on the practice team whose purpose was to help the varsity team prepare for upcoming games. Rudy practiced hard and poured his heart into each football practice. His dedication and hard work earned the respect of his coaches and teammates. During the last game of his senior year, he was allowed to play defense in the final few minutes of the game. Just like he always had done in practice, Rudy put everything he had into the game and he successfully tackled the quarterback. Rudy's teammates were so proud of him that they carried him off the field in celebration amidst cries of "Rudy! Rudy! Rudy!"

Clearly, Rudy seemed like a person who could successfully delay gratification. He spent years working hard to achieve his goals and he certainly didn't expect immediate results—he only saw a few minutes of actual playing time in a single football game.

But just because he could work hard and persevere in some areas of his life didn't mean Rudy was immune to the lure of instant gratification. In 2011, he was charged with securities fraud after the Securities and Exchange Commission revealed he participated in a "pump-and-dump" scheme. Rudy had created a company that manufactured a sports drink called "Rudy." However, the SEC discovered Rudy and the other owners of the company had made false claims about the success of their business in an attempt to raise stock prices so they could sell their shares at inflated prices. Although he never admitted guilt, he did settle. Ultimately he was forced to pay over $300,000 in fines.

The man who was once hailed as a hero for his hard work and perseverance fell prey to a get-rich-quick scheme just a few decades later. Rudy's story shows how strong our desire to stay the course can be at certain times in our lives and how quickly we may be willing to throw in the towel at other times or areas of our lives. Forgoing instant gratification requires constant vigilance. Here are some strategies to help you delay gratification and prevent you from expecting immediate results:

- *Keep your eyes on the prize.* Keep your end goal in mind to stay motivated on the days when you feel like giving up. Remind yourself of your goal in creative ways. Write down what you want to accomplish on a note and hang it on the wall or make it your computer screensaver. Visualize yourself meeting your goal each day and it will help you stay motivated.

- *Celebrate milestones along your journey.* You don't have to wait until you reach your goal before you celebrate your accomplishments. Instead, create short-term objectives and celebrate when you reach each milestone. Even something as small as going out to dinner with family can help you acknowledge your progress along the way.

- *Create a plan to resist temptation.* There are always opportunities to give in to immediate gratification. If you're trying to lose weight, there will be sweet treats to throw you off your diet. And if you're trying to stick to a budget, nice toys and luxuries will always be there to tempt you. Create a plan ahead of time that will help you steer clear of temptations that may throw you off course and prevent you from becoming successful.

- *Deal with feelings of frustration and impatience in a healthy manner.* Some days you will feel like giving up, questioning whether you should continue. Just because you feel angry, disappointed, and frustrated doesn't mean you should quit. Instead, find healthy ways to cope with those feelings and expect that they will be part of the process.

- *Pace yourself.* No matter what you're doing, you'll be at risk for burnout if you expect immediate results. Pace yourself so you can be methodical in your attempts to move toward reaching your goals. Learning the value of a slow and steady pace can help you gain patience and ensure that you're on the right track rather than rushing as fast as you can to get what you want.

DELAYING GRATIFICATION MAKES US STRONGER

James Dyson's journey began in 1979. When he became frustrated that his vacuum cleaner lost suction, he set out to build a better vacuum cleaner that used centrifugal force, instead of a bag, to separate the air from the dirt. He spent five years building prototype after prototype—over five thousand in all—until he was satisfied with the product.

Once he had created a vacuum cleaner he believed in, his journey was still far from over. He spent several years trying to find a manufacturer who was interested in licensing his product. When it became clear that the current vacuum manufacturers just weren't interested in his vacuum cleaners, Dyson decided to open his own manufacturing plant. His first vacuum cleaner went on sale in 1993—fourteen years after he began working to create his first concept. His hard work certainly paid off, however, when the Dyson vacuum became the biggest-selling vacuum cleaner in Britain. By 2002, one in four British households owned a Dyson vacuum cleaner.

If James Dyson had expected to build a successful business overnight, he likely would have given up long ago. But his patience and perseverance paid off. Over three decades later, he sells vacuum cleaners in twenty-four countries and he's built a company that sells more than $10 billion in products each year.

Reaching your full potential requires you to demonstrate will-power to resist short-term temptation. The ability to delay getting what you want now so you can get more later is instrumental to success. Here's what the research says about the benefits of delayed gratification:

- Self-discipline is more important than IQ when it comes to predicting academic success.

- College students' self-control scores correlate with higher self-esteem, higher grade point averages, less binge eating and alcohol abuse, and better interpersonal skills.

- The ability to delay gratification is associated with lower rates of depression and anxiety.

- Children with high self-control have fewer mental and physical health problems, fewer substance-abuse problems, fewer criminal convictions, and greater financial security as adults.

Whether your goal is to save enough money to go on vacation next year or you're devoted to raising children who will become responsible adults, establish realistic expectations for yourself and don't expect to see results tomorrow. Instead, be willing to commit to the long haul and you'll increase the chances that you'll be able to reach your goals.

TROUBLESHOOTING AND COMMON TRAPS

It's likely that you have some areas of your life where it's easy to create realistic expectations. Perhaps you're willing to go back to college with the understanding it will take years before you're able to graduate and earn more money. Or maybe you're willing to invest money into your retirement account with the understanding that you'll allow it to grow for thirty years. But there are also likely to be areas of your life where you want things to happen immediately. Maybe you don't want to wait for your marriage to get better or you don't want to give up the foods you love, despite warnings from the doctor. Look for those areas in your life where you can improve and focus on finding strategies to help you develop the skills you need to make slow but steady progress.

WHAT'S HELPFUL

Creating realistic expectations about how long it will take to reach your goal and how difficult it will be

Finding accurate ways to measure your progress

Celebrating milestones along your journey

Coping with negative feelings in healthy ways

Developing a plan to help you resist temptation

Pacing yourself for the long haul

WHAT'S NOT HELPFUL

Expecting that you'll see instant results

Assuming that if things don't get better right away, you're not making progress

Waiting until you get to the end of your journey to celebrate

Allowing your frustration and impatience to affect your behavior

Predicting that you have enough willpower to resist all forms of temptation

Looking for shortcuts so you can avoid the work necessary to reach your goal

CONCLUSION
MAINTAINING MENTAL STRENGTH

Increasing your mental strength isn't about simply reading this book or declaring that you're tough. Instead, it's about incorporating strategies into your life that will help you reach your full potential. Just like you need to work to maintain your physical strength, mental strength requires ongoing maintenance. And there is always room for improvement. If your mental muscles aren't being maintained or strengthened, they'll begin to atrophy.

No one is immune to making mistakes and having bad days. There will be times when your emotions get the best of you, times when you believe thoughts that aren't true, and times when you engage in self-destructive or unproductive behavior. But those times will grow fewer and farther between when you're actively working to increase your mental strength.

COACH YOURSELF

Just like any good coach should provide a combination of support and advice to help you get better, be willing to do that for yourself. Look at what you're doing well and build on your strengths. Identify areas that need improvement and challenge yourself to get better. Create opportunities for growth but understand that you'll never be perfect. Try to improve a little each day by following these steps:

- **Monitor Your Behavior**—Look for times when your behavior sabotages your efforts to build mental strength; for example, repeating the same mistakes, shying away from change, or giving up after the first failure. Then identify strategies to help you behave in a more productive manner.

- **Regulate Your Emotions**—Be on the lookout for times when you're feeling sorry for yourself, fearing calculated risks, feeling like the world owes you something, fearing alone time, resenting other people's success, or worrying about pleasing everyone. Don't allow those types of feelings to hold you back from reaching your full potential. Remember, if you want to change how you feel, you have to change how you think and behave.

- **Think About Your Thoughts**—It takes some extra effort and energy to really evaluate your thoughts. But overly positive or exaggeratedly negative thoughts will influence how you feel and behave and can interfere with your quest for mental strength. Examine whether your thoughts are realistic before determining a course of action so you can make the best decisions for yourself. Identify beliefs and thoughts that will hold you back, such as those that encourage you to give away your power, waste energy on things you can't control, dwell on the past, or expect immediate results. Replace them with more realistic and productive thoughts.

Just like a good trainer at the gym encourages a healthy lifestyle outside of the gym, being a good coach means you'll need to create a lifestyle conducive to building mental strength. It's impossible to build mental strength if you're not taking care of yourself physically. Not eating right and not getting enough sleep make it difficult to manage your emotions, think clearly, and behave productively. So take steps to ensure that you're creating an environment that will set you up for success.

Although acquiring mental strength is a personal journey, you don't have to go it completely alone. It's hard to become your best self without help from other people. Ask for help when you need it and surround yourself with supportive people. Sometimes, other people can offer tips and strategies about what helps them and you may be able to apply those to your life in a way that helps you along your journey. If you find that your friends and family aren't able to provide you with the type of support that you need, seek professional help. A trained counselor can assist you in your efforts to create change.

As your mental strength increases, you'll become more aware that not everyone is as interested in increasing their mental strength. Clearly, you can't force anyone else to change his or her life, that's up to that individual. But rather than complain about people who aren't mentally strong, commit to being a healthy role model for others. Teach your children how to be mentally strong because clearly, they're not learning these skills in the outside world. But if you work on striving to be your best, people around you, including your children, will take notice.

FRUITS OF YOUR LABOR

Lawrence Lemieux is a Canadian sailor who competed in two Olympic Games. He'd been sailing since he was a child, and in the 1970s he fell in love with solo racing. He worked hard to improve his skills and he began racing competitively. In 1988, he traveled to the Seoul Olympics, where the chance of earning a medal looked promising.

On the day of the race, the conditions were quite challenging. Strong winds combined with fast-moving ocean currents made for unusually large waves. Despite the challenges, Lemieux took an early lead. But the eight-foot waves made it impossible to see the fluorescent buoys that outlined the course and he missed one of the markers. He was forced to backtrack to the buoy he'd missed before resuming his spot in the race. Despite being slowed down, he managed to maintain second place and was still a strong contender for a medal.

As he continued back on course, however, he spotted the Singaporean two-man team's overturned dinghy. One man was badly injured and clinging to the hull, and the other man was drifting away from the boat. Given the conditions of the sea, Lemieux knew that this man could easily float away before he was rescued by a safety boat. Despite decades of training for this one goal, Lemieux gave it all up within a split second. Without hesitation, he turned his boat around and rescued the Singaporean sailors and waited with them until the Korean navy safely picked them up.

Lemieux resumed the race, but it was too late for him to win a medal. He finished in twenty-second place. At the awards ceremony, the president of the International Olympic Committee awarded Lemieux with the Pierre de Coubertin medal for sportsmanship for his self-sacrifice and courage.

Clearly Lemieux's self-worth wasn't dependent on the fact that he had to win the gold medal to feel like a success. He didn't feel as though the world—or the Olympics—owed him anything. Instead, he was mentally strong enough to live according to his values and do what he felt was right, even if it meant he wouldn't be able to reach his original goal.

Developing mental strength isn't about having to be the best at everything. It also isn't about earning the most money or achieving the biggest accomplishments. Instead, developing mental strength means knowing that you'll be okay no matter what happens. Whether you're facing serious personal problems, a financial crisis, or a family tragedy, you'll be best prepared for whatever circumstances you encounter when you're mentally strong. Not only will you be ready to deal with the realities of life, but you'll be able to live according to your values no matter what life throws your way.

When you become mentally strong, you will be your best self, have the courage to do what's right, and develop a true comfort with who you are and what you are capable of achieving.

REFERENCES

CHAPTER 1

Denton, Jeremiah. *When Hell Was in Session*. Washington, DC: WND Books, 2009.

Emmons, Robert, and Michael McCullough. "Counting Blessings Versus Burdens: An Experimental Investigation of Gratitude and Subjective Well-Being in Daily Life." *Journal of Personality and Social Psychology* 84, no. 2 (2003): 377–389.

Milanovic, Branko. *The Have and the Have-Nots: A Brief and Idiosyncrative History of Global Inequality*. New York, NY: Basic Books, 2012.

Runyan, Marla. *No Finish Line: My Life as I See It*. New York, NY: Berkley, 2002.

Stober, J. "Self-pity: Exploring the Links to Personality, Control Beliefs, and Anger." *Journal of Personality* 71 (2003): 183–221.

United Nations Development Programme (2013). *Human Development Report 2013*. New York, NY.

CHAPTER 2

Arnold, Johann Christoph. *Why Forgive?* Walden, NY: Plough Publishing House, 2014.

Carson, J., F. Keefe, V. Goli, A. Fras, T. Lynch, S. Thorp, and J. Buechler. "Forgiveness and Chronic Low Back Pain: A Preliminary Study Examining the Relationship of Forgiveness to Pain, Anger, and Psychological Distress." *Journal of Pain*, no. 6 (2005): 84–91.

Kelley, Kitty. *Oprah: A Biography*. New York, NY: Three Rivers Press, 2011.

Lawler, K. A., J. W. Younger, R. L. Piferi, E. Billington, R. Jobe, K. Edmondson, et al. "A Change of Heart: Cardiovascular Correlates of Forgiveness in Response to Interpersonal Conflict." *Journal of Behavioral Medicine*, no. 26 (2003): 373–393.

Moss, Corey. "Letter Saying Madonna 'Not Ready' for Superstardom for Sale." MTV. July 17, 2001. http://www.mtv.com/news/1445215/letter-saying-madonna-not-ready-for-superstardom-for-sale/.

Ng, David. "MoMA Owns Up to Warhol Rejection Letter from 1956." *LA Times*. October 29, 2009. http://latimesblogs.latimes.com/culturemonster/2009/10/moma-owns-up-to-warhol-rejection-letter-from-1956.html.

Toussaint, L. L., A. D. Owen, and A. Cheadle. "Forgive to Live: Forgiveness, Health, and Longevity." *Journal of Behavioral Medicine* 35, no. 4 (2012): 375–386.

CHAPTER 3

Lally, P., C.H.M. van Jaarsveld, H.W.W. Potts, and J. Wardle. "How Are Habits Formed: Modelling Habit Formation in the Real World." *European Journal of Social Psychology*, no. 40 (2010): 998–1009.

Mathis, Greg, and Blair S. Walker. *Inner City Miracle*. New York, NY: Ballantine, 2002.

Prochaska, J. O., C. C. DiClemente, and J. C. Norcross. "In Search of How People Change: Applications to Addictive Behaviors." *American Psychologist*, no. 47 (1992): 1102–1114.

CHAPTER 4

April, K., B. Dharani, and B.K.G. Peters. "Leader Career Success and Locus of Control Expectancy." *Academy of Taiwan Business Management Review* 7, no. 3 (2011): 28–40.

April, K., B. Dharani, and B.K.G. Peters. "Impact of Locus of Control Expectancy on Level of Well-Being." *Review of European Studies* 4, no. 2 (2012): 124–137.

Krause, Neal, and Sheldon Stryker. "Stress and Well-Being: The Buffering Role of Locus of Control Beliefs." *Social Science and Medicine* 18, no. 9 (1984): 783–790.

Scrivener, Leslie. *Terry Fox: His Story*. Toronto: McClelland and Stewart, 2000.

Stocks, A., K. A. April, and N. Lynton. "Locus of Control and Subjective Well-Being: A Cross-Cultural Study in China and Southern Africa." *Problems and Perspectives in Management* 10, no. 1 (2012): 17–25.

CHAPTER 5

Exline, J. J., A. L. Zell, E. Bratslavsky, M. Hamilton, and A. Swenson. "People-Pleasing Through Eating: Sociotropy Predicts Greater Eating in Response to Perceived Social Pressure." *Journal of Social and Clinical Psychology*, no. 31 (2012): 169–193.

"Jim Buckmaster." Craigslist. August 12, 2014. http://www.craigslist.org/about/jim_buckmaster.

Muraven, M., M. Gagne, and H. Rosman. "Helpful Self-Control: Autonomy Support, Vitality, and Depletion." *Journal of Experimental Social Psychology*, no. 44 (2008): 573–585.

Ware, Bronnie. *The Top Five Regrets of the Dying: A Life Transformed by the Dearly Departing*. Carlsbad, CA: Hay House, 2012.

CHAPTER 6

"Albert Ellis and Rational Emotive Behavior Therapy." REBT Network. May 16, 2014. http://www.rebtnetwork.org/ask/may06.html.

Branson, Richard. "Richard Branson on Taking Risks." *Entrepreneur.* June 10, 2013. http://www.entrepreneur.com/article/226942.

Harris, A.J.L, and U. Hahn. "Unrealistic Optimism About Future Life Events: A Cautionary Note." *Psychological Review,* no. 118 (2011): 135–154.

Kasperson, R., O. Renn, P. Slovic, H. Brown, and J. Emel. "Social Amplification of Risk: A Conceptual Framework." *Risk Analysis* 8, no. 2 (1988): 177–187.

Kramer, T., and L. Block. "Conscious and Non-Conscious Components of Superstitious Beliefs in Judgment and Decision Making." *Journal of Consumer Research,* no. 34 (2008): 783–793.

"Newborns Exposed to Dirt, Dander and Germs May Have Lower Allergy and Asthma Risk." *Johns Hopkins Medicine,* September 25, 2014. http://www.hopkinsmedicine.org/news/media/releases/newborns_exposed_to_dirt_dander_and_germs_may_have_lower_allergy_and_asthma_risk

Rastorfer, Darl. *Six Bridges: The Legacy of Othmar H. Ammann.* New Haven, CT: Yale University Press, 2000.

Ropeik, David. "How Risky is Flying?" PBS. October 17, 2006. http://www.pbs.org/wgbh/nova/space/how-risky-is-flying.html.

Thompson, Suzanne C. "Illusions of Control: How We Overestimate Our Personal Influence." *Current Directions in Psychological Science,* no. 6 (1999): 187–190.

Thompson, Suzanne C., Wade Armstrong, and Craig Thomas. "Illusions of Control, Underestimations, and Accuracy: A Control Heuristic Explanation." *Psychological Bulletin* 123, no. 2 (1998): 143–161.

Trimpop, R. M. *The Psychology of Risk Taking Behavior (Advances in Psychology).* Amsterdam: North Holland, 1994.

Yip, J. A., and S. Cote. "The Emotionally Intelligent Decision Maker: Emotion-Understanding Ability Reduces the Effect of Incidental Anxiety on Risk Taking." *Psychological Science,* no. 24 (2013): 48–55.

CHAPTER 7

Birkin, Andrew. *J. M. Barrie and the Lost Boys: The Real Story Behind Peter Pan.* Hartford, CT: Yale University Press, 2003.

Brown, Allie. "From Sex Abuse Victim to Legal Advocate." CNN. January 7, 2010. http://www.cnn.com/2010/LIVING/01/07/cnnheroes.ward/.

Denkova, E., S. Dolcos, and F. Dolcos. "Neural Correlates of 'Distracting' from Emotion During Autobiographical Recollection." *Social Cognitive and Affective Neuroscience* 9, no. 4. (2014): doi: 10.1093/scan/nsu039.

"Dwelling on Stressful Events Can Cause Inflammation in the Body, Study Finds." Ohio University. March 13, 2013. http://www.ohio.edu/research/communications/zoccola.cfm.

Kinderman, P., M. Schwannauer, E. Pontin, and S. Tai. "Psychological Processes Mediate the Impact of Familial Risk, Social Circumstances and Life Events on Mental Health." *PLoS ONE* 8, no. 10 (2013): e76564.

Watkins, E. R. "Constructive and Unconstructive Repetitive Thought." *Psychological Bulletin 134*, no. 2 (2008): 163–206.

CHAPTER 8

Ariely, D., and K. Wertenbroch. "Procrastination, Deadlines, and Performance: Self-Control by Precommitment." *Psychological Science* 13, no. 3 (2002): 219–224.

D'Antonio, Michael. *Hershey: Milton S. Hershey's Extraordinary Life of Wealth, Empire, and Utopian Dreams*. New York, NY: Simon and Schuster, 2006.

Grippo, Robert. *Macy's: The Store, The Star, The Story*. Garden City Park, NY: Square One Publishers, 2008.

Hassin, Ran, Kevin Ochsner, and Yaacov Trope. *Self Control in Society, Mind, and Brain*. New York, NY: Oxford University Press, 2010.

Hays, M. J., N. Kornell, and R. A. Bjork. "When and Why a Failed Test Potentiates the Effectiveness of Subsequent Study." *Journal of Experimental Psychology: Learning, Memory, and Cognition* 39, no.1 (2012): 290–296.

Moser, Jason, Hans Schroder, Carrie Heeter, Tim Moran, and Yu-Hao Lee. "Mind Your Errors. Evidence for a Neural Mechanism Linking Growth Mind-Set to Adaptive Posterror Adjustments." *Psychological Science* 22, no. 12 (2011): 1484–89.

Trope, Yaacov, and Ayelet Fishbach. "Counteractive Self-Control in Overcoming Temptation." *Journal of Personality and Social Psychology* 79, no. 4 (2000): 493–506.

CHAPTER 9

Bernstein, Ross. *America's Coach: Life Lessons and Wisdom for Gold Medal Success: A Biographical Journey of the Late Hockey Icon Herb Brooks*. Eagan, MN: Bernstein Books, 2006.

Chou, H.T.G., and N. Edge. "They Are Happier and Having Better Lives than I Am: The Impact of Using Facebook on Perceptions of Others' Lives." *Cyberpsychology, Behavior, and Social Networking* 15, no. 2 (2012): 117.

Cikara, Mina, and Susan Fiske. "Their Pain, Our Pleasure: Stereotype Content and Shadenfreude." *Sociability, Responsibility, and Criminality: From Lab to Law* 1299 (2013): 52–59.

"Hershey's Story." The Hershey Company. June 2, 2014. http://www.thehersheycompany.com/about-hershey/our-story/hersheys-history.aspx.

Krasnova, H., H. Wenninger, T. Widjaja, and P. Buxmann. (2013) "Envy on Facebook: A Hidden Threat to Users' Life Satisfaction?" 11th International Conference on Wirtschaftsinformatik (WI), Leipzig, Germany.

"Reese's Peanut Butter Cups." *Hershey Community Archives*. June 2, 2014. http://www.hersheyarchives.org/essay/details.aspx?EssayId=29.

CHAPTER 10

Barrier, Michael. *The Animated Man: A Life of Walt Disney*. Oakland, CA: University of California Press, 2008.

Breines, Juliana, and Serena Chen. "Self-Compassion Increases Self-Improvement Motivation." *Personality and Social Psychology Bulletin* 38, no. 9 (2012): 1133–1143.

Dweck, C. "Self-Theories: Their Role in Motivation, Personality and Development." Philadelphia, PA: Psychology Press, 2000.

Mueller, Claudia, and Carol Dweck. "Praise for Intelligence Can Undermine Children's Motivation and Performance." *Journal of Personality and Social Psychology* 75, no. 1 (1998): 33–52.

Pease, Donald. *Theodor SUESS Geisel (Lives and Legacies Series)*. New York, NY: Oxford University Press, 2010.

Rolt-Wheeler, Francis. *Thomas Alva Edison*. Ulan Press, 2012.

"Wally Amos." Bio. June 1, 2014. http://www.biography.com/people/wally-amos-9542382#awesm=~oHt3n9O15sGvOD.

CHAPTER 11

Doane, L. D., and E. K. Adam. "Loneliness and Cortisol: Momentary, Day-to-Day, and Trait Associations." *Psychoneuroendocrinology* 35, no. 3 (2010): 430–441.

Dugosh, K. L., P. B. Paulus, E. J. Roland, et al. Department of Psychology, University of Texas at Arlington. "Cognitive Stimulation in Brainstorming." *Journal of Personality and Social Psychology* 79, no. 5 (2000): 722–35.

Harris, Dan. *10% Happier: How I Tamed the Voice in My Head, Reduced Stress Without Losing My Edge and Found Self-Help That Actually Works—A True Story*. New York, NY: It Books, 2014.

Hof, Wim, and Justin Rosales. *Becoming the Iceman*. Minneapolis, MN: Mill City Press, 2011.

Kabat-Zinn, Jon, and Thich Nhat Hanh. *Full Catastrophe Living (Revised Edition): Using the Wisdom of Your Body and Mind to Face Stress, Pain, and Illness*. New York, NY: Bantam, 2013.

Larson, R. W. "The Emergence of Solitude as a Constructive Domain of Experience in Early Adolescence." *Child Development*, no 68 (1997): 80–93.

Long, C. R., and J. R. Averill. "Solitude: An Exploration of the Benefits of Being Alone." *Journal for the Theory of Social Behaviour*, no. 33 (2003): 21–44.

Manalastas, Eric. "The Exercise to Teach the Psychological Benefits of Solitude: The Date with the Self." *Philippine Journal of Psychology* 44, no. 1 (2010): 94–106.

CHAPTER 12

Cross, P. "Not Can but Will College Teachers Be Improved?" *New Directions for Higher Education*, no. 17 (1977): 1–15.

Smith, Maureen Margaret. *Wilma Rudolph: A Biography*. Westport, CT: Greenwood, 2006.

Twenge, Jean. *Generation Me: Why Today's Young Americans Are More Confident, Assertive, Entitled—and More Miserable Than Ever Before.* New York, NY: Atria Books, 2014.

Twenge, Jean, and Keith Campbell. *The Narcissism Epidemic: Living in the Age of Entitlement.* New York, NY: Atria Books, 2009.

Zuckerma, Esra W., and John T. Jost. "It's Academic." *Stanford GSB Reporter* (April 24, 2000): 14–15.

CHAPTER 13

Duckworth, A., and M. Seligman. "Self-Discipline Outdoes IQ in Predicting Academic Performance in Adolescents." *Psychological Science*, no. 16 (2005): 939–944.

Dyson, James. *Against the Odds: An Autobiography.* New York, NY: Texere, 2000.

Goldbeck, R., P. Myatt, and T. Aitchison. "End-of-Treatment Self-Efficacy: A Predictor of Abstinence." *Addiction*, no. 92 (1997): 313–324.

Marlatt, G. A., and B. E. Kaplan. "Self-Initiated Attempts to Change Behavior: A Study of New Year's Resolutions." *Psychological Reports*, no. 30 (1972): 123–131.

Moffitt, T., et al. "A Gradient of Childhood Self-Control Predicts Health, Wealth, and Public Safety." *Proceedings of the National Academy of Sciences*, 108 (2011): 2693–2698.

Mojtabai, R. "Clinician-Identified Depression in Community Settings: Concordance with Structured-Interview Diagnoses." *Psychotherapy and Psychosomatics* 82, no. 3 (2013): 161–169.

Norcross, J. C., A. C. Ratzin, and D. Payne. "Ringing in the New Year: The Change Processes and Reported Outcomes of Resolutions." *Addictive Behaviors*, no. 14 (1989): 205–212.

Polivy, J., and C. P. Herman. "If at First You Don't Succeed. False Hopes of Self-Change." *The American Psychologist* 57, no. 9 (2002): 677–689.

"Ramesh Sitaraman's Research Shows How Poor Online Video Quality Impacts Viewers." UMassAmherst. February 4, 2013. https://www.cs.umass.edu/news/latest-news/research-online-videos.

Ruettiger, Rudy, and Mark Dagostino. *Rudy: My Story.* Nashville, TN: Thomas Nelson, 2012.

Tangney, J., R. Baumeister, and A. L. Boone. "High Self-Control Predicts Good Adjustment, Less Pathology, Better Grades, and Interpersonal Success." *Journal of Personality*, no. 72 (2004): 271–324.

"2014 Retirement Confidence Survey." EBRI. March 2014. http://www.ebri.org/pdf/briefspdf/EBRI_IB_397_Mar14.RCS.pdf.

Vardi, Nathan. "Rudy Ruettiger: I Shouldn't Have Been Chasing the Money." *Forbes.* June 11, 2012. http://www.forbes.com/sites/nathanvardi/2012/06/11/rudy-ruettiger-i-shouldnt-have-been-chasing-the-money/.

ACKNOWLEDGMENTS

There are many people who have assisted me in the creation of this book.

I'd like to start by thanking Cheryl Snapp Conner who was instrumental in helping me spread the word about mental strength. It's likely that Cheryl's willingness to share my work garnered the attention of my incredible agent, Stacey Glick. Stacey believed in this project from the very beginning and I'm grateful for her assistance throughout each step of the process.

I want to thank my editor, Amy Bendell, and her assistant editor, Paige Hazzan, for their wise input and writing suggestions.

I'm grateful to my friends and acquaintances who graciously allowed me to interview them and share their personal stories: Alicia Theriault, Heather Von St. James, Mary Deming, Mose Gingerich, Peter Bookman, and Lindsey Turner.

I also want to thank my friends and family members who have supported me. A special thank you goes to my lifelong friends Melissa Shim, Alyson Saunders, and Emily Morrison, who encouraged me to share my story. Additionally, Emily's writing insights and editorial assistance were much appreciated. I'm also grateful for my coworkers at Health Access Network for supporting my writing endeavor.

I'd also like to thank my husband Stephen Hasty, the most patient person I know, for all he's done to help make this book a reality. And finally, I'm grateful to my parents Richard and Cindy Hunt, my sister Kimberly House, and all the other past and present role models who inspire me to want to become better.

23/1/15

CAERLEON